To Laura and ?

who like to

START WITH A LA

Love,

Liz

START WITH A LAUGH

An Insider's Guide
to Roasts, Toasts,
Eulogies, and
Other Speeches

LIZ CARPENTER

with
Sondra Williamson Runnells

EAKIN PRESS ⟨EP⟩ Austin, Texas

FIRST EDITION
Copyright © 2000
By Liz Carpenter
Published in the United States of America
By Eakin Press
A Division of Sunbelt Media, Inc.
P.O. Drawer 90159 ⬭ Austin, Texas 78709-0159
email: eakinpub@sig.net
⬛ website: www.eakinpress.com ⬛
1   2   3   4   5   6   7   8   9
1-57168-411-5 HB
1-57168-412-3 PB

Cover photograph by Matt Lankes

Library of Congress Cataloging-in-Publication Data

Carpenter, Liz.
    Start with a laugh : an insider's guide to roasts, toasts, eulogies, and other
speeches / Liz Carpenter ; with Sondra Williamson Runnells.
        p.   cm.
    Includes index.
    ISBN 1-57168-411-5 — ISBN 1-57168-412-3 (pbk. : alk. paper)
    1. Speechwriting. 2. United States—Politics and government—1945-1989—
Anecdotes. 3. United States—Politics and government—1989—Anecdotes.
I. Runnells, Sondra Williamson, 1951–   II. Title.
PN4142.C37   2000
808.5'1--dc21
                                                            00-058737

This book is dedicated to

my mother, Mary Elizabeth Robertson Sutherland,

who taught me the love of words and poetry,

and to

Lady Bird Johnson,

who pulled back the

national curtain for me.

Contents

Acknowledgments

Writing is a joint task—I lean on everyone within reach. Trained as a reporter, I ask questions about how to make the contract, how to play to the audience, how to market the book when it is finished, and how to entice friends and bookstores to invite me for a personal appearance.

So, before I go a word further, I have some people to thank profusely:

Sondra Runnells is an organizer, as well as a journalist. Besides the fact that she is kind, patient, and brings the best muffins for our morning progress meetings, she also is dedicated, speedy, and understands deadlines. She has contributed a number of things that I lack: organization, research, and a fresh approach to fifty years of speaking. She has made it happen in a remarkably short period of time, which is vital to someone who's my age.

Bert Pluymen is the author of *The Thinking Person's Guide to Sobriety* and a lawyer—a good one. His attention to the details of the contract was essential in bringing about my deal with the publisher, **Ed Eakin**, who is the founder and guiding spirit of Eakin Press. Ed really wanted my book, and it was Bert who made the deal.

Stephanie McKim is a very likeable young woman who knows how to fill my blind spots on a Macintosh, a PC, and the Internet. She also knows how to cook, which came in handy when I forgot that I had asked four people to lunch.

Cecilia Derkits filled Stephanie's essential role as a first reader and editor. She teaches freshman composition at Southwest Texas State University. Her willingness to read, guide, and laugh along with my copy spurred me on and saved me time.

Melissa Roberts is a top-notch, capable editor for Eakin Press. She liked the book from the start and was accessible by phone and carrier pigeon when I needed her.

Virginia Messer makes it happen at Eakin Press, and I am grateful for her prompt replies to my questions.

Jennifer Hill is Austin's hottest promoter, and her suggestions opened the doors all along the way. She'll phone anyone in Hollywood, Hong Kong, or Hondo, Texas, to book authors for appearances.

Dr. Jayme Huff was willing to "be my legs" for chores, legal and illegal.

Cathy Bonner is a longtime friend and a majordomo of the Women's Museum: An Institute for the Future in Dallas, Texas. It was her invitation to sell my book at the museum's gift store that began putting cash register figures into my mind.

Barbara Sutherland, my niece, and **Matt Lankes**, her son—two of my favorite kinfolk—pitched in when I needed help in a hurry. Barbara proofread the text, and Matt came through with his professional photography.

You, the people . . . God loves you, and so do I.

*Long before angels were stylish, I
believed in them. My mother was
an angel and still guides me, brushes
near me when I need her. I find angels
near the places of my life: the springs
of Salado, the rambling houses in Austin,
the press galleries of Washington, and
the cathedral grounds where I married,
saw my children christened and my
husband eulogized by loving friends.
Angels seldom have failed me, even
when I was handed words at the end
of one president's life and the entrance
of another's. Angels were there.*

*In writing this book, my angels were
alive—young women who wanted the
book to happen because they believed
in it and in the new women leaders
of tomorrow.* —L. C.

58 WORDS HEARD 'ROUND THE WORLD

The most important speech I ever wrote was penned as I was speeding across Dallas toward *Air Force One* on November 22, 1963. A few hours later, the new president of the United States, Lyndon B. Johnson, delivered it almost verbatim, and those 58 words were heard 'round the world.

I can't really say I wrote it; God was my ghostwriter.

As we left Parkland Hospital, we began to absorb the shock of President Kennedy's assassination and the realization that he was dead. I was aware that I was the only writer in our party and that, within the next few hours, LBJ would need to have a few appropriate words ready to deliver to the media and to the nation.

So, I pulled out a card from my purse and scribbled some words. I have always believed that they were handed to me by the same unseen hand that seemed to shepherd us all in the days ahead, as we moved from one task to another.

❧ x ❧

When I boarded *Air Force One*, its cabin was filled with a weighty, stunned silence, broken only by mournful sobs of members of President Kennedy's staff. I could not bear to disrupt the somber tone with the clatter of a typewriter, so I block-printed 58 words on a card and gave them to LBJ, who was on the phone to the attorney general, Bobby Kennedy, asking where he should be sworn into office—in Dallas or in Washington. Bobby would check and call back. Then, a call to the president's mother, Rose Kennedy, and many more calls to summon the Cabinet and congressional leaders. Anguishing minutes and hours passed.

After a few hours, we arrived at Andrews Air Force Base in Washington. A special truck with an elevator was being pulled up to the rear of the plane, and steps were attached at the front. Both doors were opened. LBJ instructed the Johnson staff to wait in the plane until the casket was lowered into the waiting hearse and Mrs. Kennedy had deplaned. When the time came, Lady Bird and LBJ walked down the stairs into the blinding lights of the media and its cameras. The new president walked slowly to the bank of microphones and made his statement as Mrs. Johnson took her place beside him.

I still am chilled reading those words, even nearly 40 years later.

Remarks Given by
President Lyndon B. Johnson
Washington, D.C., November 22, 1963:

This is a sad time for all people. We have suffered a loss that cannot be weighed. For me, it is a deep personal tragedy. I know that the world shares the sorrow that Mrs. Kennedy and her family bear. I will do my best. That is all I can do. I ask for your help and God's.

BOLD BEGINNINGS

The first time I ever appeared in public was in first grade, when my classmates and I were beginning to be aware that there were other countries in the world. Our assignment was to give a recitation on any country we chose, and mine was Japan. My mother, a poet at heart, wrote a verse for me and dressed me in a little kimono for the occasion. I walked to the middle of the stage and recited it:

> *I come from Japan,*
> *A funny little land*
> *Where people wear kimonos in the street.*
> *They have straight black hair*
> *And they never use a chair,*
> *But they sit right down on their feet.*

With that, I bowed and sat down on my feet.

I have made thousands of speeches since then— so many that, from time to time, I am asked to speak at workshops geared toward training people to be engaging speakers. I have plenty of thoughts on the subject, having started my speechmaking career five decades ago as an amateur who was thrust into the role of speechwriter and speechgiver by fate.

I have spoken about my experiences as a White House spokesperson, as an advocate for women's causes and candidates, as a humorist, and for that almighty inducement—money. I have spoken for love, for a massage, and, at Christmastime one year, for a group of German women who agreed to fill my freezer with goodies, including a lot of cookies with too many consonants in their names. At age 80, I still speak—now, from the pulpit of a wheelchair—but I limit my commitments to about 20 speeches per year, and I have become decidedly less flexible about the form of my compensation.

The speeches I give run the gamut, from eulogies and tributes at the funerals of friends and notables plucked too soon from our midst, to introductions of another speaker (the pre-speech speech, I call it—an art in and of itself), to speeches dedicating buildings (even if they're not named after me), and always, always speeches to help raise money for candidates, for breast cancer research, for a friend in need.

Whenever I speak, I'm amazed at the number of women—and men—who want advice on speaking to various groups. Some just want reassurance—it's hard to get up in front of 300 people you don't know (or you do!) and talk for 20 minutes, if you're not a natural microphone-grabber, as some of us are. But a lot of people want real advice: How do I begin a speech? What if my audience doesn't get it? When do I hit them up for the donation? What if I freeze? Should I try to memorize my speech or read from notes? And on and on.

There is a growing demand for good speakers and,

particularly, women speakers. More and more women are active in organizations that require them to make presentations, to emcee a benefit or some other formal event, to introduce guest speakers, to prepare and present committee reports, and so forth. My mail (voice-, e-, carrier pigeon-, and otherwise) is full of earnest inquiries from eager would-be speechmakers who are hungry for a reference that gives concrete advice and guidance on writing and presenting speeches.

On the pages that follow, you'll find excerpts from speeches that I consider to be among the best that I've ever delivered, each for a different occasion or purpose. I'll tell you how and why the speech worked and offer a set of tips to help you give one in the same spirit. You'll also find a section that offers solid, hard-won advice about speechmaking: sure-fire formulas, how to use humor in every speech to charm your audience and put them (and you) at ease, how to avoid being trite (or worse, dull!), how to gauge the length of your speech, how to deliver it without sounding like a robot. Also there are liftable quotes, helpful tips, and anecdotes from more than 50 years behind the podium.

The types of speeches selected for this book include:

- **Humor is Therapy**. I am a cancer survivor, and each year I am called on to speak at a fundraiser for breast cancer research. These invitations come because I know firsthand what it's all about, because I always give a comical speech (there already is enough sadness in these folks' lives), and because I never charge for a speech on cancer—I consider it bad luck. In this case, the giver is the receiver. I always get a standing ovation and come away with a great sense of wellness.

- **Using the Humor of Presidents—From George Washington to Bill Clinton**. This chapter includes a collec-

tion of anecdotes accumulated over a lifetime of research, as well as personal associations with 11 presidents and their speechwriters. My own experiences
while heading a White House Humor Group for LBJ are
discussed too. The anecdotes can be used by any
speaker.

- **Dedicating a Building or Public Monument**. For this
  sort of speech, a little research pays off big-time,
  whether you dig up details about the person whose
  name will be burnished on the building forever or learn
  more about the reason for the tribute. Often, one dramatic glimpse may say it all. Included here are
  speeches that I gave at the dedication of the Frances
  Perkins Building in Washington, D.C., and at my birth-
  place in Salado, Texas.

- **Roasts, Toasts, and Introductions**. I've probably given
  more roasts, toasts, and tributes in my lifetime than
  any other kind of speech. I've had the privilege of holding Walter Cronkite's feet to the fire, of teasing Helen
  Thomas about her (literal) attachment to the telephone,
  and of introducing former President Jimmy Carter. I've
  chosen to share all three with you.

- **Eulogies**. Eulogies are among the most difficult speeches
  to give, I think, even though they usually are blessedly
  short. I try hard to remember the essence of what a
  person has brought into our lives and to offer as many
  personal details as I can. Everyone appreciates hearing
  all those details about someone they have lost.
  Included in this section is my eulogy for Bella Abzug,
  the determined feminist and congresswoman from New
  York, as well as examples of eulogies for relatives and
  close friends.

- **Welcome to Texas**. Frequently, I am asked to welcome

various groups or organizations to Texas. Whether welcoming them to your hometown, to your new headquarters, or to a convention, this one has to be all things to all people: upbeat... funny... boosterish, even. To illustrate this occasion, I've featured my "Bragging on Texas" speech, which I gave to welcome the San Francisco Chamber of Commerce to Austin. Rather than offer the usual fare—a dull litany of sightseeing spots—I worked hard to compare our two cities, to find great things to say about San Francisco and still to have Austin come out on top. In spite of this comical portrayal of one-upmanship, I received a standing ovation from the San Franciscans.

- **Speeches to Senior Groups**. We all know that our country's senior population is growing rapidly, so it's only right that those of us who are on the far side of 65 lend a guiding hand to those who are timidly (or belligerently, in some cases!) testing the waters of seniordom. I have spoken at two national conventions of AARP, Elderhostel's 20th anniversary, and at a number of state gatherings and senior group events. Always, I use laughter as the medicine that cures the aches and pains of aging, and my observations about the advantages of being an antique are received with understanding.

- **Commencement Speeches**. Speaking to an auditorium full of graduates, whether they are departing high school or college, is a difficult assignment because they are a tough audience. It's the kind of assignment that strikes fear in the heart of the most seasoned speechmaker.

- **The Expanding World of Women**. I have always been inspired by the courage and tenacity of the great leaders of the women's movement, from the earliest suffragettes like Susan B. Anthony, Elizabeth Cady Stanton, and Lucretia Mott, to contemporary leaders like Betty Friedan, who founded the National Organization for Women in 1966 and continues to work for human rights and equality of the sexes. Throughout the years, I have been an active crusader for women's rights myself, and in this chapter I share some of the speeches that I've given to advance that cause.

- **Speeches for Worthy Causes**. When the goal of your speech is to raise money, you have to know how to kid your audience into giving, whether the cause is your local Little League team, a political candidate, the arts, or medical research: "Now, I don't want you to be like the congregation when the preacher came to summer camp meetings. The makeshift collection plates were tin pie pans. Some would drop pennies in one-by-one to sound like they were generous givers. Our preacher was wise to them and said, 'Pennies sound pretty, but they don't fold!'"

- **Tips for Speaking to High-Tech Groups**. Whether you are writing remarks for a high-tech executive or addressing a group of "techies" yourself, this type of speech is a challenge. The language of this industry, by nature, is cold and uninspiring, but that doesn't mean that your speech has to be. Many high-tech executives are realizing that they need to refine the public's impression of them as wealthy and distant if they are to extend their successes for the long term. Even a company that is an overnight success must win the support of stockholders and lawmakers. The smart high-tech executives are using speechwriters to help soften their images, humanize them, and help them to be warmly received as members of the community.

This book is organized not only for easy reading but also for quick reference. I envision it taking its place on the speechwriter's desk between Webster and Roget. For the reader who wishes to explore the book from cover to cover, each chapter explains my philosophy about a particular aspect of speechwriting and includes either the full text or excerpts from some of my own speeches that illustrate my theories. Those who wish to use the book for quick reference can turn to Part II for a compendium of speechwriting dos and don'ts, a collection of inspiring and funny quotes for using in your own addresses, questions to ask in advance of delivering the speech, and other useful material—all organized in an abbreviated format. An index of all the speeches is included at the end.

For the measly price of this little book, you will gain invaluable inside tips, interesting background on some important historical events, a laugh, maybe a tear or two, and a wealth of humorous anecdotes from political figures past and present, which you can crib at no charge!

PART I

The Speeches Speak
for Themselves

Hit 'em in the eye
with the lead—
who the hell reads the
second paragraph?
—L. C.

1

THE THREE BASIC INGREDIENTS OF A SPEECH

I have done time in both the public and the private sectors, writing and speaking for nearly half a century. Throughout my life, words have been my tools. They have led me to where things are happening, where people are exciting—first as a Washington reporter, then as a sometime-ghostwriter for Gridiron speeches, presidents and first ladies, and always on-call for friends and employers.

As a vice president of a New York-based public relations company, Hill and Knowlton, for five years, I tried to make our business clients more humane and quotable. That isn't easy with overly cautious company lawyers who kill all your quotable lines.

When you sit down to write a speech, for starters, take the advice of Helen Thomas, former dean of the White House Press Corps and my longtime friend: "Have something to say, something of merit." That may sound elementary, but many speakers have absolutely nothing to say.

Whether with good humor, personal anecdote, or lyrical vision, the speaker needs to develop an early rapport with the audience, virtually with the walk-on line.

My sure-fire formula for writing a speech goes like this:

> *Start with a laugh.*
> *Put the meat in the middle.*
> *Wave the flag at the end.*

Start with a laugh. Put the audience in a good mood and get their attention by beginning your speech with something to which both the speaker and the audience relate. And don't be stingy with the laughs—sprinkle the entire text of your speech with them. Nothing makes a point more effectively than an upbeat commentary or a funny observation about something current to you both—weather, locale, headline, or event.

Put the meat in the middle. Once you've captured your audience's attention and put them at ease, make the most of it. By this time, you should have determined what the main point of your speech will be through advance preparation: You have picked the brains of the people who invited you for insight into whom you are addressing and why. You have asked who comes before and after you in the speakers' lineup; this may furnish you with gag material. You have called two or more people from the organization and chatted with them to get a better perspective on the audience. Why did they ask you, and what message do they expect? What is the group's average age, salary, and degree of sophistication?

Then, in writing your speech, attack the subject matter in a way that reflects your own vantage point. You can make a winning impact if you "advance" your content by making two or three phone calls.

Wave the flag at the end. This is the time to inspire, to motivate, to rally the troops! It's time for the call to action, whether the action you're after is to argue a policy issue, acquire contributions, round up volunteers, or urge a letter-writing campaign. By now, you've won them over with your good nature, you've dazzled them with your command of the subject at hand, and you've engaged them with your personal perspective. Wave the colors, sound the bugle, and they'll stand up and salute!

*My mother always told us, "Try to
see the humor in the situation." So,
I learned early in life that humor
diverts, energizes, and heals.*

—L. C.

2

HUMOR IS THERAPY

Laughter has always been a big part of my life. I suppose that my appreciation for laughter and gags started with growing up in a hilarious family, spirited by a good-humored mother who was trying to write poetry while raising a houseful of obstreperous kids. My mother always told us, "Try to see the humor in the situation." So, I learned early in life that humor diverts, energizes, and heals.

That premise has served me well throughout this century. Certainly, as a journalist covering the political scene, I was surrounded by ridiculous situations. Today, as one of the few standing liberal Democrats left in Bushwhacked, Texas, I have to laugh a lot. And in the face of illness or the constant process of aging, laughter is vital in those anxious moments of apprehension and anxiety. Of course, everybody has to handle their anxieties in their own way, but "trying to see the humor in the situation" has always been the best way for me.

My mother's advice even came to me at her funeral. I was feeling very sad when I called on the florist to order the floral spray for the casket. The florist said brightly, "We've just received an order of 'Better Times roses.'" I knew that was a message from my optimistic mother, and it eased my pain.

Every year I am invited to speak to a group of my sister cancer survivors at a fundraiser for breast cancer research. I am called on repeatedly to speak to this group, not only because I have been there and survived, but also because I pepper my comments liberally with humor. If ever there was a group that needs to be able to laugh, it's this one.

Here's how I began a speech I delivered at a luncheon for breast cancer survivors:

BREAST CANCER SURVIVORS' GROUP
Austin, Texas, November 5, 1999

Many of my friends, like me, are in the "parts department." An ear here, a bosom there, and so forth. Recently, I shared the stage in Houston with Phyllis Diller at a benefit for the Battered Women's Center. She and I are the same age, but with all her tucks and lifts, she looks 50. I told her so: "You look fabulous, Phyllis." She responded with a confession: "Liz, there are no two parts of me that are the same age!"

As we speak, I am down to one of everything.

Then I told them about my own personal experience with cancer, more than a decade ago, and how humor helped me through that ordeal:

My second book, *Getting Better All the Time*, was
rolling off the presses, and I was planning a talk show
schedule and assembling a wardrobe to go forth and sell
my book coast to coast to anyone with vital signs and $18.

Suddenly, that nagging little tinge that had been
occurring in my right breast now and then became a lump.
After a trip to the doctor and a mammogram — actually,
two or three of them at my insistence because I thought
the first mammogram had lied — I faced the unwanted
fact that I had a malignancy that had to be removed.

All of this enveloped me like a dark cloud, and no
power on heaven or earth (and believe me, I called on
both) was going to change the necessity for an operation.
Still, I would not give up trying to change the verdict.
I called every contact I had developed through years of
working as a reporter and in the White House, trying to
find someone to give me another answer. I called the
Mayo brothers in Rochester, M.D. Anderson in Houston,
a recommended place in Cleveland, and even a Christian
Science friend who leans heavily on Mary Baker Eddy.
Yes, for seven days I named myself chairman of the
arrangements committee to avoid the operation.

It was sheer hell, fighting the inevitable, wondering
why this cursed thing had to happen to me and interrupt
my rollicking lifestyle. My new doctor, a surgeon, was
startled as I battered him with questions: "Who is the
anesthetist — is he a Democrat? After all the ugly things
I've said about Republicans, I certainly don't want to go
under ether with anyone else." He was disgusted. "We
haven't used ether in 20 years. And, yes, I'll get you a
Democrat."

The date was set — January 20 — and the doctor, wise
to my politics, even promised to make it at 11:00 A.M.
when Bill Clements was being sworn in as governor of

Texas, so I could pretend it hadn't happened. As my son, Scott, later said, "Mom, you only lost your breast. Mark White lost his ass."

Actually, it was a Republican friend who calmed me down. The night before the operation, while I lay there in my misery, my son said, "Betty Ford is on the line."

Someone in Washington had run into her daughter, Susan, and told her about my dilemma. Betty and I had worked together on several lost battles before. We both had lobbied state legislatures to ratify the Equal Rights Amendment. We had old ties from an old battle. And I have found that these survival ties bind forever.

Lying there in my torment, I heard Betty's voice on the telephone, saying to me, "Liz, I guess you are getting lots of advice right now." And I was—big slice or little slice? To be or not to be—reconstructed?

"Follow your own instincts. Have faith in your doctor. Accept this as a challenge. You've had challenges before, and this isn't all that much. It's another day in your life. Use your sense of humor. And, Liz, call on the strength of women like me who have gone before. I will be calling the hospital to check on you."

What a marvelous woman! I think she makes a practice of calling people to give them strength.

Meanwhile, on to the operating room.

The next morning, off it came, even as Bill Clements was sworn in as governor. In the four days in the hospital that followed, I learned the big lesson that we all learn from despair: a new appreciation and respect for simple acts of friendship and love. Those of you who have known this experience know how much those expressions of friends and family mean.

I am still in awe of how creative people can be with kindnesses.

After the operation, on Valentine's Day, a woman in Austin whom I had always admired for her pretty face showed she had great perception, too. She brought me a beautifully wrapped Valentine's gift. It was a breast. She had had the same operation 30 years earlier, and so she had a surplus number of them lying around. I never had been given a breast before, but she knew that I might want to try one out before I went shopping for my own. I will never forget it.

A friend in landscaping, Ken Wendler, came over and planted the area outside my bedroom window, around my Jacuzzi, with a profusion of ornamental winter plants, so I would have a happy view.

Another friend who is a gourmet cook prepared a meal. It would have been better if it hadn't been breast of chicken, but you can't win them all.

But the one that tops them all—no pun intended—is the letter I received from Elvira Crocker, a funny friend in Washington:

Dear Liz,

I was sorry to hear about your surgery, but from what I hear, the operation did not affect your walking and hasn't stopped you from talking. All in all, you've still got a lot of body going for you. Now, it is true that men will not be able to say, "You have great knockers or boobs," but what the hell? It's not much of an achievement. I do have an important question to ask, something that has nagged at me. All of my life, I have heard people say "a tit for a tat." But I've never known what that meant. End this mystery for me now. What the hell is a tat, and did you get one?

———————————— ►═╫═╫═◄ ————————————

This perfect upbeat ending left everyone laughing. But there are other ailments besides breast cancer. In speaking to groups over 60 years of age, it's safe to assume that many are familiar with health problems and check-ups, so I sprinkle the speech with familiar medical experiences that both the audience and I share.

———————————— ►═╫═╫═◄ ————————————

GENERAL HEALTH SPEECH — TEXAS HOSPITAL AUXILIARIES
Dallas, Texas, June 8, 1993

At my age, I have more doctors than parts. Time has taught me that you don't get a private interview when you have a check-up. I went to a famous clinic recently and spent one day posing for the x-ray machine (which must have been the longest photo opportunity ever given) head to toe. It was revealing. I have the heart of a 30-year-old, the lungs of a deep-sea diver, and the left ankle of a 109-year-old woman.

It was my local ankle doctor who introduced tape recorders into my medical life. He was young enough to be my grandson. As a matter of fact, I knew his father and his grandfather. Well, he gets on this tape recorder like he is talking to all three television networks and CNN and gives the most boring, insulting description of my condition, talking right there to my face. "Mrs. Carpenter is obese, with boggy synovium in the left ankle. Films show degenerative changes involving the left ankle with joint space narrowing and hypertrophic changes, particularly along the tibial and fibulal joints on the left."

"For God's sake," I told him, "is that all? Can't you say something flattering, like 'a dynamic, sexy woman who lives life to its fullest?'" He was back on the machine in an instant: "Mrs. Carpenter *says* she is a dynamic, sexy woman."

Talk about not sticking your neck out!

I have never talked about this publicly, but I do think I picked up Dutch Elm disease during my years in the White House. As you all know, Lady Bird was big into planting anything. We planted both at daybreak and by moonlight. One day, when I learned that we were about to plant her 247th tree, I complained: "Not another tree-planting ceremony! My limbs have begun to ache. My roots have begun to disintegrate, and I may be the first human to get Dutch Elm disease." Mrs. Johnson had a cure. She said, "Don't worry, Liz, we'll prune you and spray you, and you'll be blooming again before you know it!"

Which brings me to everyone's common health problem—aging. Everyone is into it. That sex symbol, Paul Newman, is 75 years old now. I was so glad to hear that. Cary Grant was still giving lectures at 80. He had lost his hearing, but he could talk, and give a memorable toast:

Here's to the ability
To have the agility
To take your virility
Into your senility

Actually, I learned a lot from doctors and hospitals ever since I wrote *Getting Better All the Time*, and found out I wasn't. I was 65 then and now, at 72, I realize that I owe the public an apology for acting like the golden years are just one adventure after another. I mentioned this to a friend, and she said, "Don't apologize. Write a sequel and call it 'I lied.'"

Laughter is vital, as the vital signs fade.

Once the French philosopher Voltaire was asked if he ever used humor in his speeches. "No, I never make ha-ha," he said. I have known eleven presidents, and I never met one who didn't need a little "ha-ha."
                                              —L. C.

3

USING THE HUMOR OF PRESIDENTS—FROM GEORGE WASHINGTON TO BILL CLINTON

All of us have our personal stories on how we got into the speechwriting business. For me, it happened during the Johnson years—that's LBJ, not Andrew.

One morning, when I arrived at my office in the White House to tackle my assignment as press secretary for Lady Bird—a task that included handling questions on women, dogs, and old brocades—there was Jack Valenti, waiting: "I just left the president, and he asked me to bring you his speech for the White House Correspondents Dinner. He said, 'Tell Liz to sex it up, and get it back to me tomorrow.'"

Now, LBJ didn't mean "sex" as we have come to know it six administrations later. What he meant was "get me some jokes, put in some laugh lines."

It had been a rough week, and I knew I could never produce enough humor single-handedly to cover all the gaffs that had unfurled over the past few days. As I recall, a U.S. Navy ship had fired mistakenly on another ship in the Korean harbor, the Air Force had lost a hydrogen bomb off the coast of Spain, and LBJ had sent our Ambassador Angier Biddle Duke to swim the waters to prove they were safe. Not to mention that—once again—LBJ had lifted his dog up by the ears. *Heeelp!*

So, I created what became the "White House Humor Group" and invited half a dozen people whom I considered to be fairly funny. We met late each Thursday afternoon in my office in the East Wing. Our humor efforts were enhanced by a leftover speechwriter from Fiorello La Guardia's and Franklin Roosevelt's days—the incomparable Ernest Cuneo—who always arrived with a bottle of expensive Scotch crammed into his briefcase. We then

became increasingly creative as we sipped and discussed how to make light and laughter out of the day's grim headlines. Those were some of the happiest days of my life—to the best of my memory.

Don't underestimate the value of groupies straining for laugh lines. The alumni of this group all have gone on to bigger things. Peter Benchley went on to write *Jaws*. None of us thought he was very funny, but he was kin to people who were. Harry Middleton became director of the LBJ Library. Jack McNulty was snapped up to be vice-president of General Motors. Ervin Duggan became president of PBS. And Ben Wattenberg is now with the American Enterprise Institute. I am the only one who is still straining—now over Geritol—to write funny speeches.

You are allowed to stretch the word "humor" when you apply it to the presidency. Any political story, even a lousy joke, is funnier if it is said by a president. Some presidents have had real wit, real talent at storytelling, and the ability to see the humor in a situation. It's a lot easier on the country when they do—and on them, too.

EXCERPT FROM "THE HUMOR OF PRESIDENTS"
Chautauqua, New York, July 8, 1998

I come here a sixth-generation Texan and a political artifact. By the time I was 22, I was in wartime Washington covering Congress and the White House. For 34 years, Washington was my beat, as a reporter covering Congress, the White House, and national politics. And then, for ten or more of those years, LBJ and Lady Bird lured me down from the press galleries to campaign in 1960, and I stayed on with them until Richard Nixon's limousine rounded the corner in the Inaugural Parade on January 20, 1969 — in my opinion, a day that will live in infamy.

So, I went home and started writing my first book, *Ruffles and Flourishes*, the warm and tender story of a simple girl who found adventure in the White House. It was all of that. Washington was a kinder town then, and politics was a noble profession. The cameras went down if a senator was holding a drink in his hand or had had too many. There was more laughter. More fun than funds. We still delighted in the old gag: "Washington is the only insane asylum run by its own inmates."

Franklin and Eleanor Roosevelt were the government, the Democratic Party, and despite the outgoing Great Depression and the sounds of war, there was a jauntiness about politics and the Roosevelts: the capital city, the upturned cigarette holder, the mellow laugh, the voices of hope, and the programs that rescued the country—NYA, CCC, WPA.

First ladies were not always loved—certainly not Eleanor, but it would have been unthinkable to dig up some 15-year-old billings from a law firm and make a million-dollar investigation out of it. It should be, still.

At 75 years, I readily claim to being a hymn-singing Methodist, a foot-washing Democrat, a loving liberal, and a frontline feminist. Along with loyalty, my Washington days taught me that humor is a necessity for facing life: aging, inheriting teenagers, and the changing face of politics.

There was a time in the Bible Belt when you could run for office on a three-plank platform: paying your honest debts, saving your seed potatoes, and baptism by total immersion. It was a gentler profession, which contract politics hadn't invaded with its hired focus groups, pollsters, dirty tricks, and political handlers.

Political humor came into my life early, when Will Rogers arrived in Austin in the 1930s. For 50 cents, I went to hear him. He stood on stage—chewing gum, big cowboy hat on, twirling his rope—and told of visiting President Warren G. Harding once, at the height of the Elk Hills scandals.

"I'd like to tell you some of my latest jokes, Mr. President," Will said. "Oh, you won't have to do that, Will," said the president. "I appointed them."

Once when Will was visiting the White House, he was greeted by Mrs. Roosevelt. "Where is the president?" he asked. "Wherever you hear the laughter," Mrs. R. replied.

Good humor was a quality that served FDR well.

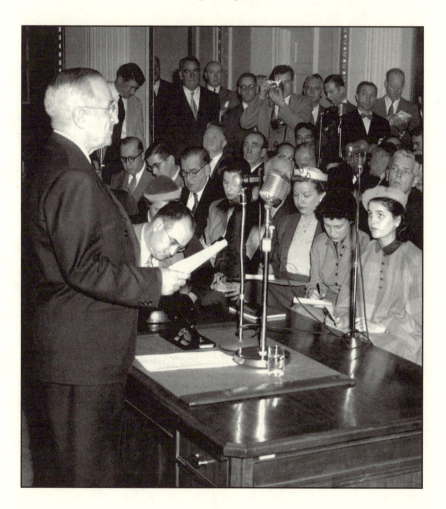

Even though humor is in short supply at the moment, we are one of the few countries that allows its citizens to laugh at its public figures.

Pretend for a moment that you are watching an Inauguration Day, as the new president steps forward and cites the oath of office:

"I do solemnly swear that I will faithfully execute the office of president of the United States with a light heart, a sense of humor and, occasionally, even an out-and-out belly laugh."

The Constitution does *not* require such an oath. The party platforms never have endorsed it. Yet, at 1600 Pennsylvania Avenue, humor is a national necessity. From "Ernest George" (who actually had a lot to smile about, being "first in war, first in peace, first in the hearts of your countrymen") to "Beleaguered Bill" (who is first in the news, first in the polls, and first in the sights of the scandalmongers), all 42 presidents have fared (or could have fared) better with a sense of humor.

Take Bill Clinton (and don't any of you say "I wish you would"). In these recent mind-boggling months, we all have gone Starr-crazy. For the life of me, I can't remember whether it was Tara Lipinski or Monica Lewinsky who won the Olympic gold medal. Or which one had oval sex in the oral office.

The president chose to ignore the allegations that ironically coincided with the announcement of a new potency drug, Viagra. That's a bad news week that demands gags! Fortunately, the president was able to muster a few laughs when he appeared before the Gridiron Club—that illustrious group of self-important journalists. His walk-on line was "And how was YOUR day? Please withhold the subpoenas until all the jokes have been told."

Or earlier, when Whitewater was hotter than sex, he

told another press dinner: "I am happy to be here. I am really delighted to be here. If you believe that, I've got some land in northwest Arkansas I'd like to show you. Your club goes back to 1944, when Franklin Roosevelt delivered his fireside chats over radio. It's not much different today, except that you insist that the president sit directly on the logs."

I can't leave the subject of Viagra without referring to another man who almost became president. It is said that Bob Dole got on the list of those to be tested for the wonder drug because, when his Japanese doctor asked him why he was depressed, he said it was "because he had lost his election."

What is clear is that good-humored politics is a bonus for the American people who are at the daily mercy of the White House, the Congress, and the Fourth Estate. America is hungry for laughter, as politics moves out of the happy-hearted hoopla days and becomes meaner and more scandalous. The president and, God knows, the people need the perspective that humor gives.

The poet Auden stated the importance best: "Among those whom I like or admire, I can find no common de-nominator. But among those whom I love, I can—all of them make me laugh."

Mark Twain said, "Against the onslaught of humor, nothing stands."

Why is humor important to people in public life? Because there is no better or faster way to smash the invisible barrier of awe that separates a president from his audience. Suddenly, he is no longer a remote, inacces-sible object. He laughs. He feels. He's a friend. Equally important, it gives him a perspective about himself. Psychologists confirm the bonding influence of laughter. It works magic in all its variety.

FDR, with his mellow smile and preppie humor, gave funny nicknames to members of his staff: Tommy Corcoran became "Tommy the Cork." Secretary of the Treasury Henry Morganthau became "Henry the Morgue."

JFK used humor to divert criticism. When he appointed his brother attorney general, he said: "I've been criticized by quite a few people for making my brother, Bobby, attorney general. They didn't realize that I had a very good reason. Bobby wants to practice law, and I thought he ought to get a little experience."

I always have been fascinated by political waggery

in the White House. So in 1963, when I moved from the press galleries to work for Vice President Johnson, I began collecting examples. I hoard them in a manuscript called "Hail to the Comic Relief." Fifteen years ago, I sold it to a British publishing house that went broke before having the chance to publish it. That required a real sense of humor on my part. Since then, I have continued to update it.

George Washington never told a lie, but even George told an occasional joke. George is best known for his exploits as a soldier, which may have been on his mind when he congratulated his old comrade-in-arms, General Henry Lee of Virginia, on his marriage: "You have exchanged the rugged field of Mars for the soft and pleasurable bed of Venus." That is George Washington humor.

John Adams was a very different bird. A lawyer and a man of letters, he was stabilized by the teasing of his wife, Abigail, and his own wry sense of humor, as recorded in their letters, which were mischievous and, well, sexy. When Abigail worried about John's health while they were separated, she wrote, "No man, even if he is 60 years of age, ought to live more than three months at a time away from his family." In reply, John wrote, "Oh, that I had a bosom to lean my head upon! But, how dare you hint or lisp a word about '60 years of age.' If I were near, I would soon convince you that I am not yet 40."

Madison was said to have told jokes that made Jefferson blush. But Jefferson—that Renaissance man—made few jokes because, his biographers contend, he was too busy being eloquent and precise.

In the annals of presidents, there were the grim ones like Millard Fillmore, whose formula for getting along in public life was to "wear a clean shirt, never swear in company and never utter a sentiment that all the asses around me don't recognize as an old friend."

Calvin Coolidge picked up on this thought with his statement: "I think the American public wants a solemn ass as a president, and I think I'll go along with them." For comic surprise among presidents, it is "Silent Cal" Coolidge who interests me most. His sparsely spoken manner and deadpan appearance gave the impression that he was more the butt of jokes than their creator.

Nothing about President Coolidge indicated that he was capable of humor. Tragedy seemed ever close at hand. His mother died when he was twelve: "The greatest grief that can come to a boy came to me," he wrote. He became president when Warren Harding died in the midst of a scandal-ridden administration. And his son, Calvin Jr., died of blood poisoning from a blister he got while playing on the White House lawn. His thin-lipped New England appearance prompted H. L. Mencken to call Coolidge "the epitome of American Puritanism, forever fretting that somewhere, someone might be having a good time." Alice Roosevelt said, "Coolidge looked like he had been weaned on a pickle," and when Dorothy Parker was told Coolidge had died, she replied, "How can you tell?"

For a tragic figure, he had amazing luck. He was the only president born on the Fourth of July. He came into office without having to run for it and escaped any tinge of the Harding scandals. His administration was prosperous and carefree, leaving the problems to his successor, Herbert Hoover. He was our best-rested president, requiring eleven hours of sleep a night— and he got them!

Ironically, Silent Cal is one of the most quoted of all our presidents. When he did speak, his words got attention. He was known for his short, tart replies. Once, when a woman approached him, saying, "Oh, Mr. Coolidge, I made a bet that I could get you to say more than two words," he replied, "You lose." Another guest introduced herself: "Mr. President, I'm from Boston." Coolidge said, "Yes, and you'll never get over it."

Without even a word, Coolidge could make total fools out of the congressional leaders, as he once did at a White House breakfast. The whole table had fallen silent for a long, painful time. Everyone waited for President Coolidge to say something. Remaining silent, he carefully poured cream and coffee into his saucer. His guests were perplexed. A few followed his example and waited for him to drink it. Instead, he bent down and put the saucer on the floor, calling, "Kitty, kitty, kitty," leaving the copycats with their saucers awash and their faces red.

Life for Woodrow Wilson would have been improved by turning aside his enemies with a flippant retort, but he memorized the poison of critics and, as Harold Laski observed, "when he was pricked, he bled." Yet, here is a man who dressed up in drag to play a joke on his bride, Mrs. Galt, on their wedding night and who, in his role as a Princeton man, recited the ditty: "My face I don't mind it, for I am behind it. 'Tis the fellow in front gets the jar."

Certainly, there must be a moment when every president feels a sense of absurdity that getting elected president "has happened to me." Well, maybe not Wilson, who believed in predestination and firmly believed that he was elected not just by the people, but by God Himself.

Tom Brokaw asked Bill and Hillary Clinton what they thought their first reaction would be when they woke up in the White House the morning after inauguration. "I think we'll probably pull the covers over our heads," said Hillary, who then dissolved into laughter.

As a fledgling nation, we were so afraid of being laughed at that political humor was risky. It took Abraham Lincoln to bring humor out of the closet. Often, he would begin a cabinet meeting by reading from the works of the humorist of the day, Ambrose Bierce.

President Lincoln was widely criticized in cartoons for his little jokes.

The story goes that when a New York congressman named Arnold called on Lincoln, he was indignant: "How can you tell your little jokes when the battlefield figures are coming in?"

With tears streaming, Lincoln flung down his book and replied, "Mr. Arnold, were it not for my little jokes, I could not endure the burdens of my country."

From Franklin Pierce, our 14th president, we hear the sense of absurdity that must sweep over every mortal who comes to that office at least once in his term.

Pierce liked to tell of learning about his own nomination. He was the last to know of it. The Democratic Convention was in a clinch and turned to Senator Pierce for its nomination on the 49th ballot. No one bothered to tell Pierce, who was summering far away in his home state of New Hampshire. By chance, his assistant, while shopping in Concord, heard the news and rushed home to tell his master: "Oh, Mr. Pierce, Mr. Pierce, ridiculous as it may seem, you have just been nominated to be president of the United States!"

You can't get nominations like that anymore. Instead, you are announced, denounced and battered all the way to the White House where, after a few days' glow, you are destined to do your best by your country in a hostile atmosphere for four or maybe eight years. There you are in that great glass house—one president, one first lady, and more than 2,000 reporters.

In the midst of last year's battering, President Clinton took a twist at his campaign slogan, "I still believe in a place called Hope," by walking onstage and facing up to what life was like: "Despite the current problems, I still believe in a place called HELL!"

The Kennedys were masters at turning the public's attitudes around. In 1960 the first primary for the presidency was in West Virginia. Hubert Humphrey, friend of farmers and coal miners, was the frontrunner. But Jack Kennedy won—big—and the rumors were that his rich papa, Joe Kennedy, had bought the election. The press carried stories on that speculation almost daily, until Jack addressed the Gridiron Club. He walked to the podium, pulling a piece of paper from his pocket. "I want to read you the telegram I received today from my father: 'Dear Jack. Don't go after Alaska or Hawaii. You don't need them, and I can't afford them.'" The result: no more West Virginia scandal.

Self-deprecating humor is a favorite technique for turning a minus into a plus. It proves you are human and makes you more acceptable.

If you read the humor of all 42 presidents, you can boil down the funniest to Lincoln, the two Roosevelts, Kennedy, Reagan, and — because I know him best — LBJ, whose antics were often more humorous than his lines. Then Clinton, for sure.

LBJ was a great mimic and a good storyteller. His humor often "just happened." When he was whistlestopping through the South in the fall of 1960, campaigning against Richard Nixon, we had a great turnout at the first stop — Culpepper, Virginia — and LBJ had a good crowd gathered around his podium at the back of the train. He got so wound up that he couldn't stop, even when Lady Bird handed him a reminder that he had 47 more stops waiting for him. He just kept talking and talking. Our timekeeper knew that we would be late all the way down the track, so he signaled the engineer to move on. This didn't deter LBJ, who kept on yelling back over the loud-speaker to the crowd, as it disappeared in the distance. "I ask you, what did Dick Nixon ever do for Culpepper?" One old gentleman who was standing near the track shook his cane and shouted back, "Hell, what did any-one ever do for Culpepper?"

LBJ was a telephone addict who never respected hours. He once called Congressman Wayne Hays at 1:00 A.M. "Did I wake you, Wayne?" he asked. "No, Mr. President," Hays replied, "I was just lying here waiting for you to call."

During the administration of George Bush, the mim-ics had a field day. Comedian Dana Carvey became a mas-ter at "Bush-speak" — incomplete sentences and talk about "the foreign policy thing."

In retirement, Bush has gotten better. I was at the

dedication of the Bush Library at Texas A&M University in College Station, along with five former first ladies and three former presidents. Bush stepped forward to introduce the foreign dignitaries who were there, among them the Japanese foreign minister—the very one that he had thrown up on when he was in Japan. Bush looked at him and said with a smile, "This time, sir, dinner is on me."

Almost every president has at least one laugh-along line to his credit. General Eisenhower is remembered for his smile, but not for many public gags. "My speechwriters keep feeding me these folksy phrases," he said. "Hell, I'm folksy enough as it is without trying to make matters worse." They must have revised their approach because that same year, Ike told them, "Those last couple of paragraphs are ringing, but I can't get away from the feeling that they make me sound like Saint Peter."

Richard Nixon tried, but generally, his humor had to

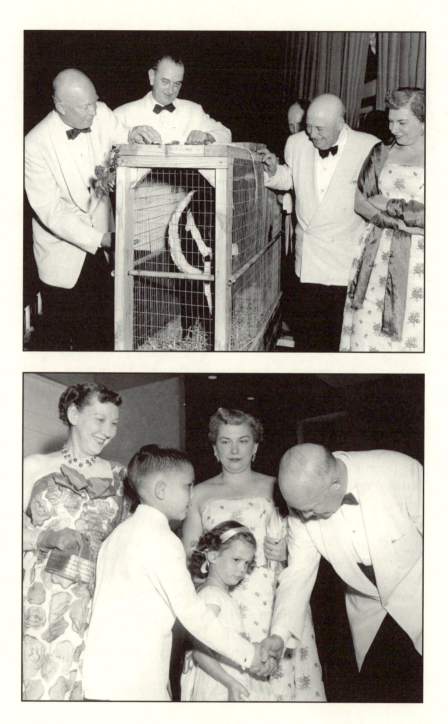

do with warning visitors against theft. When addressing groups in the State Dining Room, he would joke, "Now, don't take anything when you leave."

Even in the least funny moments, some presidents have been able to find humor. As he lay dying, James Garfield mustered a joke. Garfield was shot by a job-seeker—a man who wanted to be consul in Paris. He wrote to the president, demanding the post because he had supported him in the election. Garfield didn't agree, so the job-seeker shot him as he entered a Washington railroad station.

President Garfield lingered for two months. The doctors put him on an exclusive diet of oatmeal, which he hated. When word came to the president that Sitting Bull, the Indian war chief, was starving on his reservation, the dying Garfield said, "Let him starve." Then, on second thought, he hastily added, "No, wait! Send him my oatmeal!"

Ronald Reagan was shot as he emerged from the Statler Hotel and was immediately rushed to the hospital. He managed to walk into the operating room, where he surveyed the assembled doctors and said, "I hope you're all Republicans." His press secretary promptly gave the quote to the press, which reassured an anxious nation within minutes.

When Nancy Reagan arrived at the hospital, the president's first words to her were, "Honey, I forgot to duck."

First ladies generally save their humor and sarcasm for private consumption, but at the National Press Club, Rosalyn Carter was asked, "What is your secret for staying calm and beautiful?" Deadpanning, she replied, "Just to loaf and read the newspapers with all the great things that are written about my husband."

In all the eulogies and millions of words written about Jacqueline Kennedy Onassis, there has been scant mention of the genuine sense of humor and sly mischief of this shy, private woman. Soon after entering the White House, she issued an order that in all dispatches, press releases, correspondence, etc., she was to be referred to as "Mrs. Kennedy."

"'First lady' sounds like the name of a horse," said Jackie.

After completion of the White House's redecoration, Jackie responded to criticism of the project's high cost with her usual wry aplomb. She had the carpenters and painters reassemble the scaffolding, drop cloths, and paint buckets in the Queen's Room. Then she asked the president to come upstairs from the Oval Office. "I have something to show you," she said. When he arrived, she said, "Oh, Jack, we have to start all over again!"

After women reporters broke the barrier of the men-only Gridiron Club, first ladies were tapped to perform. A whole new talent group—Nancy Reagan, Barbara Bush, and Hillary Clinton—appeared with acts of their own to win the press over.

But their main contribution has been to be the buffer for their husbands. Never was this shown better than at the final press dinner for President Jimmy Carter. His last line was: "And now, ladies and gentlemen, I want to thank each and every one of you who has helped me during the last four years." Turning to his wife, he said, "Thank you, Rosalyn."

When he was in search of words, LBJ's practice was to exhaust every speechwriter in the process of getting the best speech possible. Huey Long thought "every man a king." LBJ believed that every man or woman was a speechwriter. He asked Dick Goodwin, from the Kennedy days, to write a speech declaring his war on poverty. It got a great response. The president quickly started sending all his speech assignments to Dick. For three months, LBJ peppered him with every assignment. Finally, Goodwin ran out of words and escaped to the Virgin Islands to replenish his brain cells. Even LBJ's long arm and telephone couldn't reach him to say, as he often did, "This is yoah president speaking."

LBJ was hurt. He brooded over the desertion for a few days. But later, riding around the ranch looking at his cattle, he was philosophical about it: "Well," he told me, "I guess a speechwriter is just like a breed bull. There are just so many shots in him."

You and I know he was right.

Always check the quotes. LBJ was so determined to make his words understood by the people that once, when he came upon a speech draft quoting Aristotle, he turned to the startled writer and said, "Aristotle? Those folks don't know who the hell Aristotle is." And he took his pen, crossed out the reference to Aristotle and wrote in, "as my dear old daddy used to say."

—L. C.

4

THE FOLKLORE OF SPEECHWRITING

Speechwriters often share with each other the instances in which they couldn't control the speechmaker. For me, the best example was when LBJ decided to trash our speech draft and use his own. He was announcing his new health legislation at the National Institute of Health on the occasion of the resignation of Surgeon General Luther Terry (best remembered as the man who took the fun out of smoking!).

In typical Johnson style, LBJ assigned the speech to two speechwriters, Douglas Cater and Ervin Duggan. They sent him draft after draft, and each one came back with suggestions for rewriting the speech. Four drafts later, the requests for revisions stopped. LBJ was happy with the speech—until an hour before he was to depart by chopper from the South Lawn.

Unfortunately, Press Secretary Bill Moyers dropped by LBJ's bedroom at 10:30 A.M. to check in. The president thrust the speech into Moyers's hands for yet another revision. Moyers dashed back to the West Wing, where he joined Cater and Duggan in churning out the final draft that literally was handed to LBJ as he boarded the chopper.

Exhausted, the three sank in front of the TV to hear their immortal words spoken by the president. They watched LBJ appear on the screen and were relieved to see that the teleprompters were in place. Then LBJ began a speech they had never heard before. It was extemporaneous, encompassing the Holy Bible, the unholy U.S. Congress, and quotations from Barbara Ward, a British author greatly admired by the president.

The audience became enthusiastic, interrupting often with tremendous applause, as LBJ quoted, verbatim, the text of the Bible verse he had heard the previous Sunday in church: "And Philip went down to Samaria and proclaimed to them the Christ . . . and the multitude gave heed . . . and they came out crying with a loud voice. Many were palsied, and many were lame, and they were healed." Obviously he had read it, stored it, and felt it appropriate for a health speech!

Back in the White House, Bill Moyers-the-Baptist threw his hand to his forehead, demanding, "How the hell did Philip of Samaria get in there?"

The more the audience cheered, the more expansive LBJ became, promising that America would wipe out cholera around the world and that, here at home, we would wipe out the common cold.

It was Johnson at his best. He not only delivered it, he *believed* it. And he was willing to use all his energy to get it done. Here was a man who had taught elocution to high school students, but who never was comfortable in front of a TV camera. Here was a man who was inspired by pressing the palm, feeling the flesh, and seeing and hearing the audience's response. If we could get him a laugh or applause early in his delivery, he was transformed instantly into eloquence—a sheer ham.

I loved it. I loved him. And I wish to heaven he was in Washington right now goading Congress, so Medicare would pick up my prescription drugs.

LBJ's speeches—written or impromptu—received so much attention that they became favorite subject matter for term themes in colleges around the country.

One day, a letter arrived for the new White House press secretary, George Christian. (Johnson went through press secretaries like a dose of salts.) The letter was from a college student.

Dear Mr. Christian,
I am using President Johnson's speech that he gave on March 31, 1968, for a term paper

in my 401 Speech class here at Northern Illinois University. There are a few questions that I hope you can answer. I do hate to bother you, but this information would aid my project greatly.

First of all, does President Johnson write his own speeches? If not, who does? What kind of background do his speechwriters have, as far as education is concerned? Do these writers adhere to any specific speech style, such as the simple, clear-cut style that Aristotle advocated or the grand embellished style that Cicero seemed to promote?

Christian passed this on to Peter Benchley, who composed the following reply:

Here are the answers to your questions:
1. All the President's speeches are written by elves.
2. The President never sees them before he delivers them.
3. The average education of the President's writers is between fourth and fifth grade. One man finished high school . . . by cheating.
4. The President's style can best be described as bombastic. He is a nut on length.

Fortunately, the response was never sent.

However, there is another rule to speechwriting that I would add: Always *check the quotes*.

LBJ was so determined to make his words understood by the people that once, when he came upon a speech draft quoting Aristotle, he turned to the startled writer and said, "Aristotle? Those folks don't know who the hell Aristotle is." And he took his pen, crossed out the reference to Aristotle, and wrote in, "as my dear old daddy used to say." (I am not making this up. It is a favorite story of Congressman Jake Pickle.)

Moving right along through Watergate to another president, I give you Gerald Ford. President Ford was the first president to hire a Hollywood gag writer, the talented Bob Orben, who had written jokes (the professional term is "special material") for half of Hollywood and a large segment of corporate America.

Watergate had forced President Nixon out of office, and the country was dismayed to learn that seven grown men in ill-fitting wigs and surgical gloves had broken into the Democratic Party's headquarters in the Watergate Building to bug it and look for campaign fodder. This was one of the more ridiculous capers in the history of Washington. It was a period to rattle not only the country, but also the new president, who had granted a controversial pardon to the departing Richard Nixon. (Not that there's anything wrong with it, as Jerry Seinfeld would say.)

The whole scenario caused such a national hubbub, it's little wonder that during the first days of his administration, President Ford couldn't walk and chew gum at the same time. He was televised stumbling down the steps of *Air Force One*. He bumped his head boarding the chopper, and he just seemed to be unsure of every step he took.

Meanwhile, *Saturday Night Live* was having a field day, with Chevy Chase mimicking the president every week. What to do? The late Senator George Murphy, a one-time song-and-dance film star who had tap-danced his way into the Senate, advised Ford: "Hire Bob Orben!"

Bob Orben not only was good at providing lines, but he also was great at setting the stage for them.

The perfect opening for Orben's debut came with an

invitation to speak at the White House Radio and TV Dinner. Orben wrote the script, persuaded Ford to rehearse it, and arranged for him to be coached on timing and the delivery of funny lines. The strategy was to offset his clumsy image by providing his own routine of gags and props that parodied himself.

By the time the Radio and TV Dinner rolled around, Ford was ready. When he was introduced, on his way to the microphone President Ford grabbed hold of the tablecloth and dragged it along with him, spilling loose cutlery, glasses, and plates in a terrible clatter. Once he reached the microphone, he dropped his alleged speech in a cascading waterfall of papers and bumped into the microphone before beginning a sophisticated patter on topical material.

The audience loved it and saluted him as a savvy new laugh-along Gerald Ford.

President Ford enjoyed it so much that, after he left office, one of the first events at the Ford Museum in Grand Rapids centered on the subject of presidential humor. President Ford emceed and Chevy Chase was the headline performer. On this occasion, they each did a parody of the other.

And the nation was once again healthier because of a president who could laugh at himself.

Like van Gogh, I believe we were not put here simply to "be happy" or to be "merely honest." I believe that we were put here to realize great things for humanity.
　　　　　　　　　—L. C.

5

DEDICATING A BUILDING OR PUBLIC MONUMENT

Dedications require *research*. You've got to dig for something that will make the difference between a dull speech that could cure insomnia and an inspiring, bring-out-the-trumpets flag-waver. I tried this when I was asked to dedicate the Frances Perkins Building in Washington, D.C. This was a thrill for me because, as a wide-eyed young reporter, I had met her and written about her press conferences in 1942. She was a feminist before the word was in our vocabulary, serving as secretary of labor from 1933 to 1945, the first woman to serve in a presidential Cabinet, and, most of all, a social reformer.

Trained as a social worker, as a young woman she worked in settlement houses in Chicago and Philadelphia and dedicated her life to improving conditions for workers.

Frances Perkins had this to say about her appointment to FDR's Cabinet:

"The door might not be opened to a woman

again for a long, long time, and I had a kind of
duty to other women to walk in and sit down
on the chair that was offered, and so establish
the right of others long hence and far distant in
geography to sit in the high seats."

By the Carter Administration, the country began to appreciate her. At the time, I was assistant secretary of education, so I was selected to speak at the dedication of the Frances Perkins Building. I was chosen for this honor because I had known her when she was in action. The speech was important to me, and I enlisted the help of my friend and colleague, Isabelle Shelton, to gather the facts.

DEDICATION OF THE
FRANCES PERKINS BUILDING
Washington, D.C., April 9, 1980

For me, it is impossible to enter this building without pausing to turn and look out over the vast expanse of the "great white marbled capital" (as Allen Drury described it) and the greensward that leads down between the government buildings to the Lincoln Memorial.

There are buildings in this city—for those of us who love it and are stirred by it—which become almost shrine-like because of the memories they embody. I believe that is what the Frances Perkins Building will be—this building dedicated to American labor, named for this remarkable, caring woman who, more than any other single individual, uplifted the face of industrial America, and forever changed the conditions of life and work for every one of us and for generations yet unborn.

As a Texan, I can't help pointing out that it was Franklin Roosevelt's first vice president, John Nance Garner, of Uvalde, who predicted to the Roosevelt Cabinet in 1933 that "the one among us most likely to some day have a monument in Washington is the Secretary of Labor — Frances Perkins."

Coming up the steps this morning from Constitution Avenue, I thought how very *right* it is that the Frances Perkins Building should be directly across the grassy Mall from the Hubert Humphrey Building. How appropriate that these two, these great consciences of social reform, should stand like sentinels, guarding the portals of the U.S. Capitol — forever reminding us of the principles of justice and equality for which they fought so valiantly.

They had something else in common, I've learned from Clara Beyer, who worked side-by-side with Frances Perkins in enforcing labor standards. Now 88, Mrs. Beyer is in the audience today. Like Humphrey, she says, Frances Perkins "sometimes lacked terminal facilities." In other words, both talked too long. But it all counted for something. They knew how to get things done. (And, I am so glad to learn from Muriel Humphrey, the two had met and liked each other instantly.)

Some of the other great names — names that are part of the Frances Perkins folklore — will join Clara Beyer and many of us at these celebrations tomorrow. They are people who knew Frances Perkins and worked closely with her. Solicitor Jerry Reilly and Associate Solicitor Tom Elliott, who between them drafted much of the landmark social legislation of the New Deal. Ewan Clague, longtime head of the Bureau of Labor Statistics, and Mary Hilton, still on the job as assistant director of the Women's Bureau. And Miss Perkins's daughter, Susanna Coggeshall — also here today.

What a loving circle of friends and colleagues!

Coming, too, is her biographer, George Martin, who had planned to spend two years writing a book about her, but became so swept up in his subject that he spent six! The other day, he wrote an inscription in his book to Clara: "Finally, here it is. I became so interested that it was six years, from start to finish, and I never grew tired of Frances Perkins. That's the test of a great person."

It was extraordinary that Frances Perkins ever came to the Department of Labor in the first place—and even more extraordinary that she was one of only two members of Franklin Roosevelt's original Cabinet still in office at the time of his death. At the offset, the old curmudgeon—Harold Ickes—was the other. William Green, of the American Federation of Labor, had declared that labor would never be reconciled to her appointment—and certainly that was true of John L. Lewis, who treated her to some of his choicest Shakespearean epithets. There also was Martin Dies, the advance man for Joe McCarthy. When he embarked upon the first of the great anti-Communist crusades, Dies ranked her on his list of "dangerous individuals," just behind Joseph Stalin and Adolph Hitler.

That may be written off as partisan invective. But she didn't fare much better, even on her own side of the fence. Rex Tugwell, who admired her, said she suffered from "a passion for veracity"—certainly a rare quality in Washington in that day, or this, and not one likely to endear the first female Cabinet member to the strong-minded men she dealt with in the corridors of power.

In his diary, Harold Ickes referred to her as "Madame Queen." William Hassett, the president's confidential secretary, borrowed from Wordsworth to describe her as "a maid whom there was none to praise and very few to love."

She didn't have much support, even among her own

kind. When Dies moved to impeach her because she refused to deport Harry Bridges, the radical labor leader,
Eleanor Roosevelt wrote: "She is alone, and I wish that
the women of this country, particularly the organizations,
could be induced to realize the true story on the whole
Bridges question. Many of the Federation of Women's
Clubs are down on Frances . . ."

She was, quite simply, the most obvious target for
any politician who sought to make headlines by hunting
a witch.

But she reinstated Franklin's teacher and Eleanor's
confidante, and when the chauvinists of that day sought
to cut her down with ridicule, those two stood behind her.
The record of her unprecedented tenure in the Cabinet is
one of efficiency and unblemished integrity.

So, you see, even long before there was women's
liberation, a woman's movement—or any of those phrases
that were part of the '70s, and so much a part of our vocabulary—Frances Perkins was stirring up a hornet's nest.

People did not understand a married woman who
called herself "Miss Perkins." They didn't understand
a well-born young woman who would spend her time
trying to salvage laborers. They didn't understand or
empathize with a woman who would pound the corridors
of the Albany statehouse—or this Capitol—and sit down
with cigar-smoking old pols to demand decent wages,
hours, and working conditions.

So, they did, alas, what came naturally to the forces
of ignorance in our land: They labeled her a Communist.

Until they met her, that is. There was the day a
group of Missouri businessmen came to see her, steaming
because the department had exposed lead poisoning in
their plants.

"How can you work for that Communist?" they said,
as they stomped around the outer office. But, when they
met Miss Perkins, it was a different story. "Where did that

woman get that reputation? She knew all about our problems," they said.

I am grateful that I came to Washington, as a very green cub reporter, in time to see Frances Perkins in action. She never knew me, but I understood her. I remember her austere, almost prim appearance, her invincible dignity. She dressed always in black, and never without the tricorn hat that I knew as her trademark, long before I arrived here. She kept the hat on even in her office—her mother once had told her it "became" the shape of her face. And there never was time to take it off.

One of the newswomen who covered her and is still around, Esther Van Wagoner Tufty, said: "She dressed rather dowdily, but as soon as you saw her face and heard her talk, you forgot her clothes, anyway."

Dr. Jonathan Grossman, this Labor Department's historian, says she deliberately cultivated the "dowdy look."

As the only woman in a largely male world, she was very conscious that she should dress very carefully—nothing low-cut, nothing flashy or flamboyant.

The image of the embattled secretary of labor that comes down to us, in any case, is that of a somewhat dowdy little lady in a tricorn hat. But that is the product of the distorted lens through which the press always viewed her. Screened out were the qualities of compassion, charm, and political savvy that enabled her to survive the alarms and excursions that attended her remarkably productive career.

Her boss, FDR, knew what she had. Once, when "Old Ironpants" Hugh Johnson was raging in the Oval Office, threatening to resign from the NRA and ride his high dudgeon down Pennsylvania Avenue, FDR whispered to Frances, "Stick with Hugh and keep him sweet."

That probably would have been beyond the capacity

of Greta Garbo, but Secretary Perkins drove the irascible general around Washington for four hours while he simmered to a low boil.

Tomorrow is the 100th anniversary of Frances Perkins's birth — we think! I believe she would have been slightly amused (with her pixielike sense of humor) that even today we are not certain whether we are celebrating her 100th anniversary (as we think we are) or her 98th.

I think it's time we gave the lady whatever she wanted. It may have been her only vanity, to never confess her age.

For many, a single moment occurs in life when history shapes you for a destiny, when you realize your obligations to mankind. For Frances Perkins, it was the Saturday before Easter, 1911 — just about this time of year. She and a friend were having tea in downtown New York when they heard the fire bells clanging, an alarm, and they rushed out to see the top floors of a ten-story building of lofts across Washington Square on fire.

The Triangle shirtwaist factory occupied the top three floors of the loft, and the employees were working overtime, turning out "Gibson Girl" shirtwaists that were the fashion. Frances and her companion saw frail young girls, already aflame, hurl themselves out the high windows, screaming as they crashed to their deaths on the pavement or impaled on an iron fence. In all, 146 lives were lost.

The fire escapes had grown too hot to stand on and eventually crashed to the ground. Many victims might have escaped to the roof, then leapt to safety on other roofs, if the doors to the stairwells had not been locked. The owner had locked them, for fear the employees might steal a few shirtwaists and, in some kind of sinister plot, drop them off the roof to waiting cohorts below.

For Frances Perkins, the fire never went out. It burned like a torch within her until her death at age 85.

From that moment, the young social worker, a descendant of the revolutionary patriot James Otis, committed her life to fighting indifference and injustice in industrial America.

For her, the memory of the charred bodies never dimmed, and all of us are the better for it. Across industrial America, the horrible tragedy seared the consciousness of the nation for industrial reform.

At the scene and throughout New York, there was a rage — a cry for reform. Instantly, New Yorkers demanded a meeting in the Metropolitan Opera House, and out of this grew the Factory Investigation Commission, created by the New York State Legislature and chaired by State Senator Robert Wagner. Assemblyman Al Smith, with whom Miss Perkins was to form a lasting political alliance, was vice chairman.

She became an investigator and expert witness for the commission. She knew the value of being an eyewitness, and she made sure each member personally experienced what it was like to work in a hot, stinking loft, crawling up rickety steps and through narrow passages — clearly deathtraps, if a single match or cigarette was dropped among mountains of cotton scraps.

But the commission's mandate extended far beyond investigating fire safety, to include sanitation, industrial disease, the safety of machinery, long hours, worker's compensation, and, eventually, even low wages.

Investigator Perkins probed them all, leading the commission to plants all over the state, where they would drop in unannounced. One visit was to a cannery where gaunt-eyed children were shelling peas at 4:00 A.M. She took them to the tenements where factory workers lived, which often were even more shocking. There, mothers who had just stumbled off the night shift, bone-tired, their faces ashen with fatigue, spent their days tending babies, cooking, and cleaning. The mothers often got only two or three hours of sleep before it was time to return to another night on the assembly line.

Bob Wagner and Al Smith, who became firm and unshakable leaders for social justice and industrial reform on the state and national scenes, got their education as members of the Factory Investigation Commission, where their persistent teacher was the determined young woman, Frances Perkins.

The flame and rage that ignited Miss Perkins that Easter Sunday afternoon now burned in them, too. They knew she was right. They knew the New York legislature and others were willing to use their clout on behalf of a social reformer.

It was the combination of the canny old pols and the dedicated young social worker who was prodding them on. It's what Representative Martha Griffiths did on ERA. It's what Carrie Chapman Catt did for women's suffrage. It's a combination that is very successful when it does happen—and thank God it's happening more and more.

It's a pattern of power that is a sure winner.

Bob Wagner, who later went on to the U.S. Senate, spearheaded passage of the New Deal's landmark National Labor Relations Act—the Wagner Act—which guaranteed workers the right to join unions and to bargain collectively.

Many of the reforms that Miss Perkins and others brought from New York to the national scene were to change the conditions under which every one of us lives and works today. They were the heart of the New Deal. And, interestingly, they were almost all contained on a scribbled list that Frances Perkins brought with her one cold day in February 1933, when Roosevelt—about to be inaugurated president in March—summoned her to his New York City townhouse to offer her the post of secretary of labor. He had not come to this decision easily or willingly.

She suspected what he might ask because there had been press speculation. And she knew that Molly Dewson—head of the Democratic National Committee's potent Women's Division and credited by many with electing Roosevelt—had said, when he offered her "anything you want," that the only thing she wanted was Frances Perkins as secretary of labor.

Four times, Roosevelt had asked Molly Dewson, and four times, she gave the same answer. Time was getting short. Frances Perkins was the last Cabinet appointment to be announced.

At first, Frances Perkins did not think it was a good idea. Organized labor was violently opposed to her. They thought the Labor Department post should go to someone in the labor movement, and they were particularly incensed that Roosevelt would even consider naming a woman.

She told FDR her misgivings, but when he insisted, she read him her list on the crumpled piece of paper. These were the issues she would push, if she went to Washington, she said—and if he did not approve of her program, he should not appoint her.

It was a courageous thing to do. It would have been so easy to take the job—and the honor of being the first Cabinet woman in history—without "making waves," as we would say today. She also needed a job, as she was her family's sole breadwinner. Her husband was institutionalized with a mental condition—a private grief that she sought desperately to conceal—and her daughter, Susanna, whom she adored, was in a private school.

The munificent Cabinet salary, by the way, was $15,000 a year, soon to be cut back to $10,000, as an economy measure.

But, it was not in her nature to take the easy way. She had a deep belief in God, and what she truly had come to believe was her "mission"—to lift the burdens of the downtrodden through intelligent, enlightened government action. Al Smith, the tough-talking, hard-nosed political tactician, had shown her the way, and she wanted to take the lessons on to the national scene. Nothing could turn her from that course.

Roosevelt accepted her program, and in time, most of it passed into law and into history — the New Deal's great social legacy, which no politician since has succeeded in dismantling, although more than one has tried.

So, my friends, never forget:

- If you were to lose your job today, you would get unemployment benefits for many weeks — thanks largely to Frances Perkins.
- If you need a job, the U.S. Employment Service will help you find one — thanks largely to Frances Perkins.
- If you are injured on the job, you get worker's compensation — thanks largely to Frances Perkins.
- Your chances of getting injured at all are greatly reduced — thanks largely to Frances Perkins. (It no longer is common for unguarded industrial machines to cut off a worker's arm or hand, as happened with distressing frequency, until the tireless crusader got some protective laws passed.)
- If you get time-and-a-half after 40 hours — which you do — that, too, is thanks largely to Frances Perkins.
- And, when you are old and no longer work, you will get Social Security — again, thanks largely to Frances Perkins.

Many others played a role in bringing all this about, of course. She would be the first to note that she never walked alone. Nor do we women in government today.

When I first came to Washington, the vast majority of women in government were working as clerks or secretaries. In the world outside, they were teachers or librarians, and not too many of those.

Today, as I walk through the government corridors, I am struck by so many women sitting at the policy tables, hammering out decisions—as assistant secretaries, deputies, general counsels, program managers, and division heads—and, of course, our two proud women Cabinet members.

I get very weary of the "superwomen" I meet occasionally, those who think that they hold these fine jobs solely because of their own brilliant qualifications. No woman does it all by herself. Those who came before her set the climate, opened the doors. There is a thread stretching from woman to woman that's beautiful—even though some of them don't know it.

But even though we've made progress, we should not delude ourselves that we have climbed all the mountains. As a people, we still have a long way to go in this country to reach the plateau of justice and equality for which Frances Perkins reached.

For women, the road ahead is particularly long. Frances Perkins, whose life was a living testament to the capability of women, would have been knocking at FDR's door if she could have seen the headline the other day that, despite some progress, women's salaries are still only 59.1 percent of those paid to men.

She would be disturbed that such a high proportion of working women still are confined to jobs as clerks and secretaries, despite the increased number of women in seats of power.

She would be distressed that, after 200 years of history, there never has been a woman on the U.S. Supreme Court. I am sure she would not rest until that was rectified. She would be thrilled, however, that President Carter has appointed 32 of the 35 women who are serving as federal judges today.

In today's world, she would be appalled by a nation that still does not have the Equal Rights Amendment an incredible 60 years after the struggle for it began, immediately after passage of the Women's Suffrage Amendment in 1920.

Frances Perkins made speeches for women's suffrage on New York street corners. If she were here today, I'm sure she would be doing the same for ERA and other unfinished items on the agenda of the American woman. She would be the first to exhort, in the words of her beloved grandmother, whom she so often quoted: "When in doubt, do what is right."

You can pay tribute to her today by making a vow within yourself that you will not rest until our unfinished business is completed.

That is the spirit of Frances Perkins—and we can do no less.

The *Washington Post* picked up the text of this speech for its op-ed page and helped spread the message.

While the Frances Perkins speech was a national event, another dedication was a personal honor when I delivered a dedication speech at Salado, Texas, during my White House years. Led by John Ben Shepperd, the great Odessa and Texas civic legend, consummate volunteer leader and organizer of the Texas Historical Marker program, the State of Texas designated the home where I grew up as an official state historical site, with a marker bearing my name. Both the first lady of the United States, Lady Bird Johnson, and Texas's first lady, Nellie Connally, were present for one of the most heartfelt occasions of my life.

ROBERTSON FAMILY HOME — DEDICATION
AS HISTORIC MONUMENT
Salado, Texas, August 25, 1967

Mrs. Johnson, Mrs. Connally —

I am deeply touched, as is everyone here, that these two sweethearts of Texas — these two remarkable women — have made this a very special day for us all.

My friends and kinsmen — sitting here, listening to the generous words of the speakers, I was greatly relieved to hear that you had come, not to bury Liz Carpenter, but to praise her.

Earlier this year, when the letter arrived telling me about the marker, I knew someone must have made a mistake. Could it be a typographical error? Hysterical marker, yes! Historical, no!

Could John Ben Shepperd, the man who has made markers a way of life, suddenly have confused me with Liz Taylor, Liz Whitney, Liz Odum? Of course, John Ben has been at this business a long time. He first earned his reputation for markers by building the pyramids for the Pharoahs, the Taj Mahal for the Taj.

Today, John Ben, you've outdone yourself. Surely this is the last of the big-time splendors.

Looking out over this sea of faces is a little like drowning. A whole lifetime passes before me — familiar faces from Bell County, Austin, the University of Texas, and Washington.

It is awkward to share in public something that is very private, but this homeplace casts a spell upon all those it has touched. For me, it always has been like rose petals in some old earthenware jar. Every corner is a memory — dozens of cousins on pallets in summertime, reading the worn old books about Anne of Green Gables or the Little Colonel, the cool dignity of the old parlor where my

mother and father were married, cleaning out the spring
so the watercress could grow free, cutting down your own
cedar tree in the back pasture for Christmas, feeding baby
lambs in the spring, your uncle saddling up the mare so
you could ride to Norwood's Store for the mail.

That's the Salado I take with me wherever I go, and
I am deeply grateful to my Aunt Lucille for the determination to see that this lovely old gem of a town was kept for
the future. Now my children and others who have known
only the sound of the city may feel the enchantment of
this spot.

My, how it looms on the map today! I remember so well 25 years ago when my husband came courting — by Greyhound bus. I had told him to watch carefully for Salado, that it was just a dot on the road. I met the bus, but no one got off. Had he missed it? No, there he sat, completely unaware this was a town. I beat on the window and said, "Get off! This is it! This is Salado!"

Today, Salado is the advance guard of restorations in Texas.

I wish all my provincial eastern friends (the most provincial region in the world) who think Texas is big hats and big talk could see our pockets of charm from the riverboat town of Jefferson to the Palo Duro Canyon.

I am so glad we are taking the time to dig around our deep roots. And what do we see? We are discovering, and we are helping the world to discover, that if we are a ten-gallon state, it is ten-gallon courage, ten-gallon compassion, ten-gallon hospitality.

This very house has a room called the Stranger's Room, built for the specific purpose of giving unknown travelers a bed for the night. It would have been easier just to let them ride on, but we are not a people who take the easiest and most expedient course.

And because I see this quality firsthand each day in the actions of the two Texans for whom I work, I must share those thoughts.

It would be easier for the president not to bother the Cabinet about hiring women, but he does, and he gets results.

It would be easier for the first lady to sit complacently in the White House, rather than take the time and trouble to walk through the classrooms of Appalachia and lend a hand to lift people out of ignorance.

It would be easier to stick to the same outdated welfare program, rather than risk the giant steps of Head Start and Job Corps to help people out of poverty.

It would be easier to do nothing about the struggle for freedom around this restless globe, rather than to stand with honor.

Thank God they do not take the easy course.

Today, I read with some embarrassment the shining marker extolling my virtues. Let me let you in on a secret: I am doing just what I love doing. If I were writing the marker for this day (a day you all have made indelible in my memory), it would read simply:

"Here stands a happy woman, blessed by an overindulgent family and overenthusiastic friends."

———— ⚡⚡ ————

In the following case, the fast-growing town of Pflugerville, Texas (located just north of Austin), suddenly had new folks and new money, so it needed a new library. With all that newness, however, I couldn't rely on local history. I drew the body of my speech from specific books and spoke about how reading enriches one's life.

———— ⚡⚡ ————

DEDICATION OF THE
PFLUGERVILLE PUBLIC LIBRARY
Pflugerville, Texas, February 13, 1999

The 21st century beckons with a friendly wave to writers. Someone—God, medical science, or Shirley MacLaine—has given us the gift of extended time. Today, we have authors—the Delaney sisters—who have written a bestseller at age 100.

Those of you who aspire to be writers face the prospect not only of more years in which to write, but also more knowledge to enrich those years and the effort that you put into them. You are here at the birth of an era when all the information of the ages can be summoned to your personal computer, to be turned—with the effect of alchemy through your own talents—into the gold that some of you will produce in the form of books, articles, and scripts. I envy you the experience, but at the same time, drawing on the memories of my own life, I want to remind you—at least those among you who may feel overwhelmed by the information explosion—that one cardinal guiding principle for writers never has changed for writers as diverse as Jane Austen, Helen Keller, or F. Scott Fitzgerald: You need look no farther than your own life to find material.

Life is literature. It provided Thomas Wolfe with the vivid characters that play so well in his novels. He turned them into a high form of literature as he scrawled his books written in longhand on top of a refrigerator because that was the most comfortable place for a man of his tall stature.

Nora Ephron, in *Heartburn,* used her own marriage-on-the-rocks to get even with a husband who, at the time, was in hot pursuit of a British ambassador's wife. You can sense her delight in her vengeance as she describes her rival's "thick ankles" in the battle for Nora's prize recipe for "sorrell soup."

Words, words, words! We are surrounded by words tonight, as well as with old friends and new ones who are contained in these volumes that widen our worlds and offer us adventure of all sorts. There is no limit to where reading can take you. On these shelves are books that will make you think and laugh and weep. Among these volumes are travel and adventure books that can lead us wherever we want to go and "how-to" books from which we can learn valuable lessons, like how to garden, knit, relax, diet, or even how to write.

We invite all of you to come back to visit this library

many times. From here, you can ride a raft down the Mississippi River with Tom Sawyer, Huck Finn, and their friend Jim, the runaway slave; you can dance with Jay Gatsby, the suave, life-loving hero of Scott Fitzgerald's famous novel *The Great Gatsby*; you can thrill to the exploits of great sports figures like Babe Didrikson, the Texas girl who, although untrained, used her natural athletic abilities to become a winner in golf, track, and the high jump; you can climb the Swiss alps with Heidi and meet her grandfather; you can listen to the wisdom of old heroes like Sam Houston, hearing him admonish us to "do right and take the consequences."

You can hear 20th century heroes like Jake Pickle tell how harrowing it was to sign up for two parades in one afternoon. Jake is a marvelous storyteller; in his book *Jake*, he takes us on a campaign ride around dozens of small-town squares, as he passes out those famous pickles of his. You can waltz through the lyrical words of Thomas Wolfe, whose tortured Eugene Gant will emerge to haunt you from the pages of *Look Homeward, Angel*.

Browse among these shelves, and you can hear Atticus Finch arguing for justice in *To Kill a Mockingbird*. Once, when I met the author of that novel, Harper Lee, someone asked her the best way to learn to write. "Read your head off" was her brief reply. That's good advice, and that is exactly what is happening here in Texas, where both reading and writing are on a roll. Our own Texas history is vivid and close at hand. Old letters and journals from the last 200 years now are being found in trunks and candy boxes that have been stored in attics across the state—vivid, real-life tales that our ancestors put aside for us to read or to write about.

Probably the very first writer in Texas was Cabeza de Vaca, who was shipwrecked in the 1500s, captured by an Indian tribe, and taken to the chief. The chief vowed to spare his life if he could save his sick and fevered son.

"Not knowing what to do, I made the sign of the cross," de Vaca wrote in his journal, telling of his travels in Texas.

A lot of us who try to write call on higher powers to send us our words. Erma Bombeck, who wrote a funny column about family life five times a week, once told me, "Every night, I say my prayers and turn my hands upward, saying, 'Please, God, send me words for tomorrow.'" I have tried that, and it works.

In all of us, there is a yearning to know who we are. It begins to prod us onward as we age and begin to research our family's genealogy, trying to capture on paper the times and events that are the sagas of our lives.

Alex Haley, author of *Roots*, said, "In all of us, there is a hunger marrow-deep to know our heritage: who we are and where we came from. Without this enriching knowledge, there is a vacuum, an emptiness and the most disquieting loneliness."

Here, in this library, you can begin your own search. You may not find all your answers, but you can spot some guideposts that will lead you onward.

James Michener did not begin writing until he was 47 years old, but before his death, he wrote more than 30 books. When he came to Texas to write about our state, he told me that as a child he grew up in Doylestown, Pennsylvania. He was an orphan, living in a foster home, and his foster mother, Mrs. Michener, read to the children every night. When the library opened in that small town, he said, "I read nearly every book in it." Many years later, when he returned to Doylestown as a famous author, the librarian told him that the first two library cards issued there were to him and to Margaret Mead.

Out of this library, I predict that there will be other Micheners and Meads who will go on to make their marks.

---

*As one of the few standing
liberal Democrats left in
Bushwhacked, Texas,
I have to laugh a lot.*
                    —L. C.

6

Using Personal Experiences to Connect with the Audience

If humor doesn't do it for the speaker, try a personal story to lure the audience.

Surfing TV one night, I came upon a good example. President Clinton was using his own experience to rally support for preservation of our national parks. He was at the Grand Canyon, and he described what it was like, as a young man, to discover true beauty.

"Thirty years ago, while driving west, for the first time, I watched the sun set over the Grand Canyon for two hours. This morning, I got up and for about an hour, I watched the sun rise over the Canyon for the first time. In both cases, watching the interplay of the changing light against the layers and colors of the Canyon left me with lifetime memories."

The president then urged the American people to follow the advice of that great environmentalist, Teddy Roosevelt, "to take the long, long look at the need for public lands."

This is a speech about communications, yesterday and today. It is a crazy sort of speech about how it was and how it is—through the eyes of a 76-year-old communicator who has seen technology change from an upright L. C. Smith typewriter in a noisy city room to a satellite feed, a silent fax, a computer, and all the fixings.

It also is a jumping-around sort of speech because that is what I have done, from girl reporter to White House correspondent, then from press secretary to vice president of a public relations firm, and, finally, to author and speaker.

The technology that now is at our fingertips makes my head spin. We can reach anyone in a helluva hurry—a matter of minutes and seconds. As someone who grew up before television, when phone numbers were four digits and almost no one phoned long distance except in case of death, it is eye opening. This ability should be bringing us closer together as a nation and as a world people, and thanks to some in the media like Ted Turner, to some extent, it is. But far too often, our technological achievements are serving divisiveness, sensationalism, and the degradation of the human spirit.

Alas, much of what we communicate does not live up to the magic of available high technology. The content of newspapers and TV is unworthy of the technology that carries it so fast, so far, and to so many. It is loud, violent, cynical, superficial sound bite stuff. It assumes that you have to stand up and yell at someone to make them listen or read. And everyone is deafened by it.

I think it is time that we, the creators of the messages, take hold and assume some responsibility for what we are parroting. We must, I think, exercise some personal discretion about the words we echo. That is the premise of what I want to say to you today, as I take you through my almost 60 years of communications.

I was 22 when I got my journalism degree in 1942, but I already had a taste of being a working journalist. I was still a student at the University of Texas when I walked into the *Austin American-Statesman* and asked for my first job.

"You don't want to be a newspaper reporter. That's the most overworked, underpaid, oversexed profession in the world!" Those were the words that the newspaper editor growled at me as I applied for my first reporting job. As I recall, he never did anything to remedy the complaints.

I was 18 at the time, eager to follow in the footsteps of the great reporters and their romantic adventures about which I had read. I hoped to go to all the magical places they told of and do all the exotic things they had done.

Some of it I have done. I have sipped champagne by moonlight at the Acropolis. I have ridden a whistlestop train through Dixie in the wake of civil rights legislation—not once, but twice. I have danced at the White House, and I have walked the pockets of poverty through Appalachia with Lyndon and Lady Bird Johnson. Me, just a simple girl from Salado, Texas.

Of course, I knew I couldn't start off that way. In the beginning, I was assigned to short features or stories about women's clubs. But I was swept up with the feeling of being in-the-know, of rubbing shoulders around the city room with the star reporters. Occasionally, after work, I was asked to come along to some nearby hangout where they drank beer and I drank Coca-Cola, but where we reflected on the shortcomings of the mayor or the governor, and where we compared leads. Comparing leads was the after-work pastime of reporters then.

In a strange way, those after-work gatherings at newspaper bars were important. They were places of camaraderie, places to laugh at the day's work, and places for dreaming. But they no longer exist except in a few press clubs and in those rare cities that still have two daily newspapers. I miss them. I have to live vicariously at Phil's Bar as I watch *Murphy Brown* on Monday night TV. Murphy, a television newswoman, is the updated version of the former hard-bitten, wise-cracking good old gal sob-sister of the '30s—the kind played by Rosalind Russell in *My Girl Friday* or in *Front Page*, the classic about yesterday's newspapers.

The excitement of the old competitiveness is gone. Most towns are single-newspaper towns, and, alas, few have a nearby newspaper bar that offers the kind of daily soul searching, philosophizing, and irreverent meeting place I seek. City rooms look corporate and high-tech—downright medicinal. No bottles in the bottom drawer. No talented old winos needing to borrow money until the next paycheck. The news staff is young and full of carrot juice. All our old bad habits are gone. Today's reporters are on a health binge. They don't drink or even smoke. After work, they head for the hike-and-bike trail or the health food markets to check the labels.

Maybe mine is a lost cause. Maybe we simply can't turn back the clock. Newspapers, like other forms of communication, no longer are the hand-crafted world of eccentrics and individuals that they used to be. Transfers of ownership to mega-corporations and high-tech production have given a sameness to the products, instead of the raw individualism that existed up through the '60s.

There is talent out there among the young writers, but space is shrinking. Newspaper copy begins to read like TV sound bites, and the layouts begin to look like the *National Enquirer*. So many elements distance communicators from their readers. The security at the reception desk, the required security badges reading "Visitor," the whole CIA atmosphere that never existed in the old days. Maybe it is necessary, but I relish the times when a citizen with a story or a complaint could drop in and talk it over. I look back on the times when an international PR firm turned down the tobacco account because it refused to hawk the industry's false information.

But that is getting ahead of my story, and I want to share with you some glimpses of what it was like to be a Washington reporter, balancing home and job.

I spent 34 years of my life in Washington, D.C., in various types of communications jobs — as a reporter covering presidents and first ladies, from Franklin and Eleanor Roosevelt on. I went there fresh from the University of Texas. It was wartime, the great white marbled monuments were dimly lit, the whole ambiance pulled me like a magnet, and I walked the halls of the National Press Building with my scrapbook of clippings, knocking on doors, looking for a job. The time was ripe, and I landed one job and then another that gave me those coveted passports to the White House press conferences and the press galleries of Capitol Hill. The world unfolded for me, great stories in the making, world leaders addressing the Congress as I leaned over the balcony to see them closer. Committee hearings with Alger Hiss, Joe McCarthy, and the return of General MacArthur.

Is there any other profession in the world that would afford a girl from Texas a front-row seat before eleven presidents and the right to question them? My stories were not the major stories. My pieces of the pie were stories about what FDR, Harry Truman, Ike, Jack, or LBJ were doing for Texas, Arkansas, or Oklahoma. My copy ran in a dozen papers in Texas, in the *Arkansas Gazette*, and in the *Tulsa Tribune*.

I loved it, and I loved working with the man I had married along the way — Leslie Carpenter, also a reporter.

I had worked with him back in high school on *The Austin Maroon* and in college on *The Daily Texan*, and finally, with World War II over, in Washington. Children we wanted, and children we got—a son, Scott, and a daughter, Christy.

There is something in the modern superwoman that wants to do everything at once—bear children, interview congressmen and senators, even dictate news stories from a hospital bed. I don't know why I thought I had to personally break the news of every new postmaster or upstream dam in the Southwest, but that is the kind of female I am.

The kids thrived on it. They grew up knowing how to write down messages from editors who were searching for Les or me. The mix of being mom and reporter, of juggling deadlines and PTA meetings is possible—if you are married to a super guy, and you talk the same language.

Well, this is too much about me, but I want you to know that I believe that women can have it all. Men do—why not us? Timing is the trick, and wanting to live fully propels you.

I feel that I've had it all—or almost all. Events kept

unfolding, and I was there as they did. I was there that dreadful day in Dallas — November 22, 1963. In a police car riding across Dallas, I scribbled the most important 58 words I ever will write — the words that LBJ spoke a few hours later when *Air Force One* landed at Andrews Air Force Base in Washington.

Suddenly, the Johnson years swept me up completely and, as Lady Bird said so eloquently at the time, "I walked on stage for a part I never rehearsed." We made the most of it, rushing to get the laws on the books for Head Start, the Job Corps, all those Great Society programs that President Kennedy dreamed and President Johnson delivered. Lady Bird traveled the country to translate the aims of those "War on Poverty" programs. The first lady, the press, and I made 47 trips to do just that. It was my job as press secretary to organize the trips and charter the plane, which, incidentally, was paid for by the press, not the public.

Those were heady days — perhaps the best times of my life, though I keep finding the best times. Like being part of the contemporary women's movement that began in 1971, and being a founder of the National Women's Political Caucus, which was created to urge women to run for office and, hopefully, win — and we are beginning to get there. Take Texas: If you don't think this is a fantastic woman-run state, you haven't walked through the State Capitol Building, the Texas Railroad Commission, the State Insurance Board, or just about any other hall of state government.

Life would have been easier if I had not gotten so deeply involved, for I poured 15 years of energy into it, and I am still at it. But I would have missed out on so much, on so many friendships with remarkable women of all income levels and education levels, as we lobbied legislatures for the Equal Rights Amendment. It has been a long struggle, but we are making progress.

I rub my eyes in wonder. Can this be me—76 years of age, sitting on my hillside in Austin with my Macintosh computer, my Hewlett-Packard printer, my Murata fax machine, and my Prodigy on-line service chirping away, blinking their red lights at me—all having problems because of a thunderstorm?

Yes, communications has come a long way, and so have I in the last 50 years. The day I realized I had was when the fax machine brought in—so silently, there on my rocky hill—a message scrawled by a friend of mine, a striving novelist from London. It took only a few seconds to reach me. She told me that she had just sold her book on Sam Houston's life to Doubleday, and her editor was Jacqueline Kennedy Onassis. I felt like Alexander Graham Bell getting the first long distance telegraph by Atlantic cable.

Which leads me back to my main point: It's time to focus on how we are making use of all of these magnificent tools, to make sure that we are using them in the best possible ways. I cannot underscore adequately the gravity of this. We, as a planet, are on an ecological and spiritual collision course with destiny. We have no time to waste. We must come together as a world people in order to save ourselves. We must learn new forms of cooperation. We must share solutions to our human problems across borders and oceans.

Communications technology is our electronic nervous system. If used to its highest ends, it can save us, or, if not, contribute to our demise. That gives those of us who are communicators a very special responsibility.

We can be the voices that wake people up, give them hope, and inspire them to be part of the solution, or we can join the cacophony of voices of despair that leaves people feeling alienated and hopeless.

There's little wonder that the American people are turned off to politics. Most of what we hear from the media is very shoddy stuff, full of cynicism and fury, signifying nothing. We begin analyzing the motive before we tell the story.

We are obsessed with repeating how dull Bob Dole is, instead of telling what the hard-working legislator is able to offer while still hanging on to the Christian Coalition that has overtaken his party.

Bill Clinton makes himself hoarse talking about unity, trying to inspire local communities to cope with "those hopeless girls with babies and angry boys with guns," but the media finds it much more fun to focus on the flaws and irrelevancies of his and his staff's behavior.

The local news is dominated by a staccato of murder and rape. Lots more is happening each day in our communities—hopeful things, amazing things are being accomplished by ordinary people—but you would never know it by most of the news coverage. Incidentally, the laziest, cheapest form of journalism is when reporters choose simply to follow the police beat. By letting it dominate, they leave their audience with nothing but fear.

I know we can do better. I know each of you can do better. Whether you are writing the news, ad copy, or creating a 30-second sound bite for a political client, you must take responsibility for the tenor of the content. Do you want to be Geraldo or Bill Moyers? Sally Jesse or one of those remarkable young women on CNN? Charles Keating or Ted Turner?

There are a few heroes in today's world of communications, such as Bill and Judith Moyers, Nina Totenberg, Roger Rosenblatt, Charles Osgood, Jeff Greenfield, Anna Quindlen, Robin McNeil, Ellen Goodman, and Charles Kuralt. Great communicators and great thinkers, all, and they share something else that is fundamental—faith in the human spirit, a belief in our capacity for goodness and greatness. Their vision is not obscured by cynicism, greed, or celebrity-seeking. Although the issues they cover are often disturbing, complex, or frightening, we are better off for having read their words and heard their voices. They illuminate the issues and events of the day and leave us more prepared as citizens to participate in the democratic process.

The attention-grabbers, on the other hand, are without conscience, and while our vast communications system should push America forward, instead it has turned America sour. It has created a lack of trust and yielded to communicating the darker side of human nature. It puts distance and fear between us. It will bring the house down if we don't exercise perspective, a sense of proportion, and get away from the superficial to what really is significant.

The world is not going to hell in a handbasket, even if that is what Geraldo and the *National Enquirer* would have us believe. We are not a world of weirdoes. It really is up to the communicators, I believe, to clean up their acts. There are extraordinary individuals and groups who are making great things happen in this country and throughout the world. You must make them happen in your own field by being innovative, committed, and responsible. When those extraordinary things do happen, it will be because people like you, who yearn to make your lives count for something, led the way.

When I received an invitation to speak to the American Bandmasters Convention, I wondered how I could establish a rapport with a group of musicians, and then I remembered that I had once played clarinet in my junior high school years. I began my remarks this way:

AMERICAN BANDMASTERS CONVENTION
Austin, Texas, March 2, 2000

Friends and kinfolk, because I have a relative out there from Arkansas — wave, wherever you are! Fellow noise-makers ...

Funny you should ask me to speak to this group of musicians. I say funny because you didn't — could not — know that once I was in a band and played the clarinet. It was back in junior high school in the '30s. I decided, because I have always believed in living at the edge, that being a member of the junior high school band would be fun. I liked the way they marched, and so I went down to a pawn shop (I am not making this up) and bought a clarinet.

The price of $32 stays in my mind, and someone found me a clarinet teacher — a Mr. Blowbaum (of course, my brothers and sister called him "Mr. Blow-bum") — and he taught me enough to pass the tryouts. I would never do that again. For one thing, I could never figure out why the clarinet had sixteen holes, when I had only ten fingers. But, as the song goes, "It was fun while it lasted ... " And so, here I am, 65 years later, able to tell about it. The high school band and, subsequently, the University of Texas band were fortunate that I decided to become a journalist instead, and they didn't have to cope with me.

My other identity with bands was when I was working at the White House and came to know the United States Marine Band — John Philip Sousa's group. There is nothing so grand as arriving in evening gown for a State Dinner and being welcomed by the red-coated Marine Band playing — well, virtually anything, such as the "Star-Spangled Banner" or "There is Nothing Like a Dame." Those men made us proud, and that, I understand, is what bands are for — to make us all proud.

Oh, yes, in traveling with President Johnson around the world, bands were very big with us. Our advance men would get to a country about a week before *Air Force One* was to land, and they would pass out hundreds of sheet music versions of "The Eyes of Texas" to the hundreds of bands, from high school to national bands, to play when the president arrived and motorcaded, hopefully, to cheering crowds along the short drive to the Capitol.

Somehow, South Korea sticks in my mind. It is about ten miles to the Capitol, and so it took about 100 bands of all types to provide the music along the way. You haven't heard band music until you have driven that parade route in the press bus right behind the president's car and heard the Korean version of "The Eyes of Texas" more than a hundred times in less than an hour.

Korea had really turned out to welcome LBJ. In fact, when we reached the Capitol, LBJ was impressed. The president of Korea mounted the stage, and while waiting for the rest of the entourage to get settled, LBJ turned to President Park and asked, "How many people were out there?" President Park turned to his assistant and reported: "Three and a half million people," adding, "I'm sorry, but that's all the people we have."

LBJ told the story often and always finished it up by saying, "All my life, I have been looking for humanity and, at last, I found it."

Now, I was told that you wanted to hear a bit more about Texas and LBJ . . .

———————————— ▪◦◦▪ ————————————

The rest of the speech had nothing to do with music or bands, but by using personal stories to identify with the bandmasters' group—no matter how remote the connection—and by injecting my own experience, they related to me and listened.

Praise can sound phony.
Lighthearted remarks and
personal anecdotes about
the subject or person bring
them to life.

—L. C.

7

ROASTS, TOASTS, AND INTRODUCTIONS

Even when the purpose of the occasion is to honor someone for his or her accomplishments or contributions, audiences get weary and suspicious of praise, praise, praise. In these instances, anecdotes are a good way to reflect on the humanity of the person being recognized. If you don't have any of your own, you can pick up anecdotes from friends of the honoree or from reading their own books.

Roasts, toasts, and introductions are the perfect occasions to use humor. In early 2000, when Cactus Pryor introduced Austin Mayor Kirk Watson at an event, he jokingly alluded to our city's burgeoning population and crowded streets: "The mayor is just back from Japan. He didn't intend to go to Japan, but he got into the traffic on I-35. . ."

Over the years, I have been asked twice to introduce my fellow reporter and good friend Walter Cronkite. The latest occasion to roast Walter was at the awards ceremony for the American Newspaper Women's Club in Washington.

ROAST OF WALTER CRONKITE—
AMERICAN NEWSPAPER WOMEN'S CLUB
Washington, D.C., May 13, 1997

What a star-studded night! When this club asked me to come to a roast of Walter Cronkite, I was flabbergasted.

"Are they crazy?" I asked myself. And the answer is, "Yes, the shining city on the hill" is self-destructing. In their media madness, they are roasting the most trusted man in America. And, certainly, the last trusted man inside the Beltway. They are aiming at the last of an endangered species—a beloved member of the working press.

Walter Cronkite is the golden-throated warbler, the spotted owl, the one-horned rhinoceros, the last trusted reporter.

Don't they know that, out in the grass roots where I live, the ratings of the media have plunged below Dick Morris?

How could you do this to Walter? The man has no flaws. He has even been married to the same woman for 56 years. Can anyone else in this room make that claim? The smart-as-a-whip Betsy Cronkite—the pretty redhead and graduate of the University of Missouri's journalism school. Walter discovered her in Kansas City and never let her go.

Roast Walter if you can, but in Texas, we genuflect!

In 80 fabulous years, he has lived the nostalgia of a profession that thrived on the rules; get it straight, get it first, write it fair. He still does it his way.

Born to the profession, at age six Walter was running around the neighborhood, shouting the news: "President Harding is dead!"

He came under the spell of a great professor at the University of Texas, which also gave journalism degrees to Lady Bird Johnson, George Christian, Bill Moyers, and me.

Maybe you remember how it was in the '30s and '40s with aspiring print journalists. We read Richard Halliburton's *Seven League Boots*—how he swam the Hellespont by day and roamed the Taj Mahal by moonlight. We wanted to do that. We wanted to be like Hildy Johnson in *Front Page* and know the suspense of a pressroom and the excitement of a breaking story.

And after work, reporters waited for the first edition at a nearby hangout and compared leads over a beer, until we could read our own copy—several times—before we read the rest of the paper.

Walter's description in his book is classic: "I suppose those dedicated to most crafts take pleasure in the sights and sounds and smells peculiar to them, but I can't imagine any being as exciting as the heavy odor of printer's ink, pulp paper and melting lead, the clanking of the old Linotype machines, the deafening din of clacking news service printers, rewrite men shouting into the old stand-up telephones—God, how I loved it!"

Little wonder he looks askance at those reporters who delve into the negative. "They'd rewrite the Book of Exodus with a car chase," he says.

If you think all this sounds antiquated, there is nothing antiquated about Walter. His love of the craft carried him from typewriter to microphone to the widening eye of the TV camera, which took him—and he took us—to the stars.

He has covered stories, big and small. In an early byline from his college paper—*The Daily Texan* of 1935—Walter interviews Gertrude Stein and declares her "genuine," despite sharp criticism because anyone who writes "a rose is a rose is a rose" must be a weirdo.

At the Chicago World's Fair, he covers Sally Rand's fans, on to Moscow's United Press Bureau, the pelting bombing of Britain, the Nuremberg trials, the space shots, the ocean plunges. His is a running story still in progress and will include, undoubtedly, a ride on a UFO to the first interplanetary interview with Timothy Leary.

The eyes of Texas (and the world) are upon you, Walter. You are the way it was and the way it ought to be.

⸻ ⊨⊨ ⸻

Another longtime friend and press colleague since 1942 is Helen Thomas, the beloved dean of White House correspondents. I jumped at the chance to introduce her when she came to Texas to talk about her memoirs.

⸻ ⊨⊨ ⸻

INTRODUCTION OF HELEN THOMAS
LBJ Library, Austin, Texas, 1999

Mrs. Johnson, friends —
I am prejudiced, of course, toward our speaker, Helen Thomas, a close friend of half a century, a colleague from my own reporting days when we both arrived in wartime Washington, very excited, very ambitious, and very, very green and, yes, I may be influenced by the fact that her book contains ten references to me, mostly favorable.

Like newswomen everywhere, I have a deep pride in her accomplishments, but I also find her book does for me what Walter Cronkite's *A Reporter's Life* did. It makes me believe in the press again, and just when I had lost faith and decided they had all gone mad with their obsession with scandal.

Now, here comes Helen Thomas, the UPI reporter at the top of her profession, dean of the White House Press

Corps, the one who says, "Thank you, Mr. President," and doesn't always mean it. Here is Helen, at 79, so in love with her job that she still arrives in the White House pressroom at daybreak, ready for whatever the president—whoever it is—has up his sleeve or on his mind.

All that pent-up personal passion that Helen has to subdue as a wire service reporter is uncorked in her book, *Front Row at the White House*, and what comes out is empathy and understanding of the men who have had to bear the burdens of the world—the presidents—and the first ladies and families she has encountered in that most important address of 1600 Pennsylvania Avenue. She tells the details, not only with the old journalism rules of who, what, when, where, and how, but also the why of them.

Tonight, I want to tell you the why of Helen Thomas. By coincidence, Helen and I arrived in Washington 57 years ago, the summer of 1942. Both of us were 22 years old, fresh out of college—she from Wayne University and me from the University of Texas—both full of excitement and energy, drawn to wartime Washington by the overwhelming desire to be where the action was. And, most certainly, that was Washington, D.C., capital of the Free World, centered by the White House of Franklin and Eleanor Roosevelt, who had lifted this country out of the Great Depression and reformed it along the way, with those alphabet agencies that breathed new life into a country of breadlines and joblessness. They brought us from fear to hope and made us, as a nation, realize that with a little help from the government, everything is possible. (I hope you Republicans are listening.)

Helen and I were fired up with determination to be reporters in that pulsating city—a city whose allure our fellow journalist Allen Drury was to describe so completely in his novel *Advise and Consent*.

"Washington takes them like a lover and they are lost," he wrote. "Washington, that great white marbled capital that stretches ... along the placid Potomac, a city that mirrors so faithfully their strange, fantastic, fascinating land in which there are few absolute wrongs or absolute rights, few dead certain positives that won't be changed tomorrow ... their wonderful, mixed-up blundering, stumbling, hopeful land in which good men do evil and evil men do good things in a way of life and government so complex and delicately balanced that only Americans can understand it, and often they are baffled."

Helen and I had arrived in that great revolving city of uniforms at a time when men were leaving for war and women were arriving for work.

I snapped up a half-reporter/half-secretary job for $25 a week. Helen remembers she failed as a waitress, so she became a copy girl at the *Washington Daily News* for $17.50 a week fetching copy and coffee for the staff, but she was dazzled by it all. In time, she moved on to the United Press to cover the Department of Justice, the Federal Communications Commission, HEW, and the White House.

She was on her way — bringing pride and distinction to parents who came as immigrants from Lebanon at the turn of the century with scant schooling themselves, but a determination to educate their nine children.

"America has a special meaning for me," she told me this summer over a weekend of reflection I will always cherish. "I don't believe in being hyphenated. We are all Americans, period."

We relished in those good old days, the thrill of the noisy pressrooms, the upright Underwood typewriters, the ringing bells signaling another big news break, for those of us who remember — today's high-tech newsrooms are much too clean, much too quiet to make our blood race.

Helen, together we have followed and recorded history in the making through eleven presidents and first ladies.

Of course, in the LBJ years, you were asking the questions, and I was answering them — or avoiding them — as we followed that remarkable lady who planted the trees and daffodils, walked the trails of the redwoods, rode the rafts down the Rio Grande and Snake rivers, and the whistlestop trains through the worried South, and danced under those chandeliers in the East Room with the father of two White House brides.

Can you believe, Helen, that we have lived 79 years of this struggling century and seen the power and the glory of this country firsthand, stood there with pad and pencil to cover the heady moments, the exhilarating successes, the deep disappointments, and the heartbreaks of public life?

Helen laughs about it, but she still believes that being a reporter is the most glamorous and romantic profession in the world, even when you are standing in the rain for four hours waiting for a news source. That's Helen.

And tonight, we are honored to have her here to tell us about it.

―――――――――――――― ◆◆ ――――――――――――――

I recently had the extreme pleasure and honor of introducing former President Jimmy Carter—a man whom I admire greatly—at a dinner honoring him and former President Gerald Ford in Austin. The occasion was the LBJ Library's Symposium on the U.S. Presidency. Let me share my remarks . . .

―――――――――――――― ◆◆ ――――――――――――――

INTRODUCTION OF
FORMER PRESIDENT JIMMY CARTER
Austin, Texas, April 12, 2000

Mrs. Johnson, Mr. President, and Mr. President—
Your dialogue today raises the presidency by 99 percent. In addition, I love you both and am grateful to you

both for what President Ford and Betty, and President Carter and Rosalyn, have done for women.

My assignment today is President Carter, but let me say at the start, because I am a political artifact, that I have admired you both from your earliest days.

The first time I met Gerald Ford was when I covered his swearing-in to Congress: a football hero and a war hero, replacing a crotchety old Dutchman—Bartel Jonkman. It was a great improvement.

Now, on to President Carter. I met him when he was governor and was entertaining a group of Democrats in the Georgia Governor's Mansion in Atlanta. Bob Strauss had maneuvered me a spot as a Democratic National Committeewoman. On entering the Mansion, Governor Carter said that his mother, "Miss Lillian," was upstairs in

bed with a bad shoulder, and he asked if I would go up to see her. I did, and I knew immediately that she was my kind of woman. She was just back from the Peace Corps in India. She said that, after her husband died, she needed to "do something," and so she told her children that she was going to join the Peace Corps.

"I thought surely one of my children would try to talk me out of it," she said. "No one did. They all said, 'Great, go for it, Mom.'"

I have children like that. I was taken aback, visualizing that this gentle, gray-haired Southern lady had been any such place.

"What did you do there?" I asked.

"Honey, I gave vasectomies, and you have no idea how grateful those men were!"

After her return to Georgia, everywhere she went, Miss Lillian was asked to tell about her experiences in the Peace Corps. She did—to ladies' organizations everywhere, including the United Daughters of the Confederacy.

Several times, I have been mistaken for Miss Lillian. We are both white-haired, short, lovable. I must tell you what happened when I was in Greece. She had been there shortly before I visited. I arrived at a big Easter-time dinner for the government officials in Athens. They had run out of seats for the guests. I must have looked around furtively because, suddenly, there appeared two official-looking men, very apologetic: "La Madre, la Madre" ("the Mother, the Mother"), they said, and escorted me to the seat next to the prime minister. No one ever knew, and I never told.

I thoroughly enjoyed being your mother for three hours. So, let me yield now to the president, philosopher, fly fisherman, Miss Lillian's (and my) son—Jimmy Carter.

On another occasion, I introduced Jake Pickle, former U.S. Congressman and a longtime news source and friend. He had written a book and was being honored by the Austin Society for the Elderly, which was bestowing on him its 1997 award for helping senior citizens.

SALUTE TO CONGRESSMAN J. J. "JAKE" PICKLE
Austin, Texas, September 26, 1997

Cactus, thank you for those words. Congratulations to you, Sister Mary Rose. I have a confession, Sister: I spent last night in bed with Jake. I called him up this morning and told him I thought his book was really great. "I was hoping for a better punch line," he said.

That's Jake, and you are going to get a real kick out of his collection of stories, just as he has gotten a real kick out of life. I am so glad his daughter, Peggy, helped to get the essence of Jake's stories into a book.

Now, unless you arrived in the 10th district in the last 15 minutes, you have already met Jake Pickle and are wearing one of his green Pickle pins. Those Pickle pins have been everywhere. Throughout the 10 counties that made up the old 10th district, they've been strewn on Congress Avenue, in old Dime Box and new Dime Box, and at the Luling Watermelon Thump when he drafted Governor Ann Richards to help him toss them to the kids. Even in saying farewell to his old partner, John Connally, Jake slipped a pickle pin into the flowers on his casket, for old time's sake. Talk about sentimental!

Life is an adventure or nothing at all. Helen Keller said that once, but Jake has been living it every day of his life.

From the day he was born in West Texas, he was a man of vision. While the mesquite and chinaberry trees, cactus and sand might look hopeless to some, he saw their potential—a habit that he practiced every day in Congress, relishing the people he served, as well as those he worked with—the big shots and the little shots.

Parades are life's blood to a politician. And Jake found a lesson from his first: Never stand behind the horses.

Parades always seem to invite disaster, but he couldn't miss one. Giddings and Kyle were staging their parades on the same day. With military precision, Jake plotted how he and Beryl could do both. But, wouldn't you know it, the Giddings parade ran late, and by the time the Pickles breathlessly reached Kyle, the parade had started, and all the convertibles had been taken. The only vehicle left was a pickup truck—a half-ton, flatbed

workingman's truck with livestock fencing. Jake hurried Beryl into the truck and hung up his posters: "J. J. Jake Pickle" on the sides. He looked for a driver. They were all taken. He yelled at a young aide to jump into the truck and drive. "Congressman, I can't drive a gear shift," the aide said. Jake couldn't believe any able-bodied Texas male couldn't operate a stick shift. Meanwhile, the parade marshal was livid. Cars behind were stacked up. The marshal yelled at them, "Get in this line, or get out."

"I can drive a stick shift," Beryl said. "I learned that when I was twelve years old." Quickly, she moved behind the steering wheel. Of course, she was wearing a dress and high heel shoes, suitable for a parade, not for driving farm equipment! She started it up. Every time she shifted or braked, she had to step on the clutch, or the truck would die. Shift, stall, jerk. Shift, stall, jerk—all the way.

"I held on for dear life with one hand and waved and threw out pickles with the other," he said.

But while we aren't here to talk about Jake's stories, they say a lot about the man who makes the most of life and who relishes the little shots and the big shots like a nurturing father.

I daresay, there is no one in this room who hasn't known a personal expression of friendship from Jake. He's always there for us—to give the eulogy for the president or for my husband, a reporter who covered him for the Austin paper.

He was way out front to see how to make a great university even greater in the 21st century. He saved Social Security, Medicare, and the Disability Act. He has been a true friend to this organization. There is nothing antiquated about Jake. When the women's movement started, he called me up to rehearse him on how to say "Ms." He learned, and won their respect and support.

Yes, Jake can fix a flat or carry a casket. He is ours, and we love him.

He has the vision to see the basic fact of life: That love, laughter, and service to your fellow humans are the ways to happiness. And so, for a happy man, the Austin Society for the Elderly happily presents you their award for 1997.

He makes the best of times out of the worst of times.

I always revel in the chance to toast one of my good friends and colleagues, partly because an occasion that calls for a toast is celebratory and attended by our mutual cohorts. Toasts are similar to roasts, although they often are shorter. The following toast, which I offered to my fellow Austinite Cactus Pryor at a Prevent Blindness dinner a few years ago, is one of my favorites:

TOAST TO CACTUS PRYOR
Austin, Texas, October 29, 1992

I could kick myself for not thinking of it sooner, but why didn't we run Cactus Pryor for president of the United States?

He has more brains than Dan Quayle. He can complete a simple sentence, which is more than you can say for George Bush. He has more ozone than Al Gore, the draft board got to him quicker than it got to Bill Clinton, and he uses more corny expressions than Ross Perot.

By gosh, Cactus picks up the hood and checks the engine. He listens to that sucking sound of jobs being pulled into Mexico and Asia—he listens with his good ear. And, unlike James Stockdale, he keeps his hearing aid going in the other. He is in one constant major state of overhaul.

Cactus thinks what this country needs is a world-class entertainer in the White House, and that's him.

Through his years as a speechmaker, Cactus developed both a foreign and a domestic policy. His foreign policy, simply stated, is that he will go anywhere in the world, as long as he doesn't have to pick up the tab. His domestic policy, simply stated, also is "no tabs, please." That's the way he has kept down his personal deficit.

In fact, he has pinched more pennies than female fannies, which is more than you can say for some of the other candidates.

Talk about tight: Cactus always watches his wallet, even on Sundays. He has a clear understanding with his pastor, Gerald Mann, that when he sings at church he doesn't have to drop anything into the collection plate.

More important is the fact that Cactus is a practiced entertainer. He knows how to fill time, and laughter is something that we could have used during the last six months of this political season. Within the last month alone, we have seen three national debates, each one lasting 90 minutes. That adds up to 270 minutes, and when you throw in all the analyses, plus Ross Perot's infomercials, we are into light years.

Frankly, I would have preferred to hear Cactus do the whole campaign solo in one of his many roles in which he dons beards, goatees, and hairpieces and fools the audience. He has appeared as a Swedish car dealer, a Russian rocket scientist, and an English gardener. Why not an American presidential candidate? Lesser men have made it.

Among the more pleasant chapters of my life associations with Cactus are the times when I played the straight woman as Lady Bird Johnson gave out her highway awards every October. We were supposed to amuse the audience—a real challenge, since it was mostly people from the Highway Department, one of the most flagrant networks of Aggie alumni. Unfortunately, this act had a longer run than Abie's Irish Rose.

Cactus would dress up in costumes in keeping with the highway theme. Once, he was disguised as a litterbug, another time as a bluebonnet. Then there was the time that he came dressed as a dead armadillo, followed the next year by his impersonation of a yellow stripe down the highway. On another occasion, still, he came as a tree with a pesky squirrel on his shoulder that kept looking for his nuts. It was after that occasion that Lady Bird moved the awards ceremony to Houston.

Of course, Cactus has entertained heads of state at the LBJ Ranch, and he once was known to make Billy

Graham laugh, until the curtain came down and the smile turned into a biblical scowl.

Well, that's Cactus. I love him, the whole state loves him, and well they should because he never has forsaken us for the big time and the bright lights. Let us lift our glasses, our flasks, our coffee cups to Cactus!

If you've walked through Washington, you've learned how to make a toast. I keep one handy for dinner parties when I'm called on to lift my glass to a lady I love. This is a standard in my supply.

TOAST TO LADY BIRD JOHNSON
Acapulco, Mexico, January 1990

What a treat to have a moment to toast my friend, my former employer, and the person who is the inspiration for beautifying America!

When I went to work as her press secretary and chief of staff in the White House, I spent six years of my life teaching reporters how to spell "pyracantha" and "azalea."

Lady Bird is a trailblazer. I am only a camp follower. But, during those exciting White House years, I can report that we literally woke up Sleeping Beauty, shook her, and marched her onto the stage and into the offices of mayors, governors, congressmen, senators, and presidents to stem the tide of asphalt and highway billboards.

Harry Middleton, besides directing the LBJ Library, writes fabulous, irreverent limericks, and tonight he is here to deliver his lyrical and loving toast:

She attended the Nation's great needs,
Was admired by Persians and Medes,
But acquired, sad to say,
Somewhere on the way
An unhealthy attachment to weeds.

In 1998 I was chosen to introduce one of this country's most esteemed poets, Maya Angelou, at the University of Texas Distinguished Lectureship series.

INTRODUCTION OF DR. MAYA ANGELOU
Austin, Texas, April 18, 1998

Words, words, words. Since her childhood in Stamps, Arkansas, Maya Angelou has been making words thunder or making them whisper. She causes you to cry and prompts you to laugh. We marvel at the plays, movies, children's books, and poetry she has written. This room is filled with students who are studying her words in their classes.

Some fans know her as a writer for Oprah Winfrey in the series, "Brewster Place." Many more heard her deliver the magnificent poem at President Clinton's inauguration.

She speaks English, French, Spanish, Italian, Arabic, and West African Fante — and Texan. More importantly, she speaks the language of the soul. Dr. Maya Angelou.

Perhaps because I am writing this book in the springtime, my fancy turns to thoughts of love, and so I include my "Toast to Love," which I have used at engagement parties, weddings, and anniversaries of people close to me.

TOAST TO LOVE

Let us lift our glasses to love:

To me, love is a moment and a lifetime. It is looking at the other and knowing that, if you don't spend the rest of your lives together, you will have missed the boat. Love is working together, growing at the same rate together. It is respect for each other and for the people about whom each of you care. However difficult, it means liking each other's relatives and friends. Love is wanting to shout each other's successes from the rooftop. Love is wanting to wipe away the tears and comfort when failure comes. Love is laughter, especially in the middle of a quarrel.

Love changes if it is normal, grows into deeper and deeper appreciation of each other. Some people need more loving and touching or more space and understanding than others. Meeting those needs is love. Love makes you reach out to humanity because caring about humanity is love. My brother Tom saluted love in a poem that I often quote:

Let us remember Love, and each his own.
Love makes the serpent equal to the God.
It makes us larger than our flesh and bone
And lifts us from our jail of time and sod.
The wine, the roses, candle, violin
Are keepsakes in the musty books we save.
The kiss, embrace, the tingling of the skin,
All these delights are shadows in the cave.
And so, the games we play, the dance and search,
The pleasure, fame, the power and promotion,
Whether at market or home, in school or church,
Are passing mists and squalls upon the ocean
Of Love that gives us life till the last breath
And dying looks with that which knows no death.

*Humor can be an effective
salve to soothe the wounds of
grieving friends and family.*
—L. C.

8

EULOGIES

In no other instances are personal experiences of life as important as they are in delivering a eulogy. Humor can be an effective salve to soothe the wounds of grieving friends and family. When they come to a funeral, people want to be lifted from the pain of loss and to celebrate a life as the deceased lived it.

I've delivered many eulogies in my life and, as odd as it may seem, I enjoyed each one of them. Preparing them gave me an opportunity to re-appreciate my own memories and to share my special experiences with others who loved them.

When Erma Bombeck, a dear friend and fellow journalist, passed away in 1996, I was honored to be asked to deliver one of her eulogies and to reuse it later when her papers were given to the University of Dayton.

ERMA BOMBECK
Phoenix, Arizona, April 1996

Erma Bombeck's laughter will always ring out for me from a hundred places where we traveled together for

more than five years, fighting to get the Equal Rights Amendment passed. We lost (for now) but what a great trouper she was for the cause.

She would recite the proposed amendment to the U.S. Constitution—"Equality of rights under the law should not be denied or abridged on account of sex"—and then add, with a grin: "Look, ladies, those 16 little words simply mean one size fits all."

We traveled every weekend to one or several of the 16 states yet to ratify the amendment and called on governors and legislators. We went by bus, motorhome, plane, and, occasionally, by foot and on bended knee. Once, in Florida, as we boarded a "see-through" helicopter, Erma leaned over and whispered, "I wish we'd worn better underwear."

In Little Rock, Arkansas, after a long day of speeches, we headed by car through a rainstorm to a late dinner. As we searched for the designated landmark—a red mailbox—I rolled the window down and stuck my head into the driving rain. "Watch those two-dollar permanents," Erma yelled. "They frizz."

Around the fire at our host's home, I asked the assembled group, "Why do we do this? After all, Erma, you could be playing tennis in Scottsdale."

She replied, "Because when my children ask me, 'What did you do in the war for equality of women, Mom?' I don't want to have to say, 'I gave at the office.'"

What an asset she was. Women poured out to see her and cheer her—white-collar and blue-collar women who knew her through her columns because she shared the problems of dishwashers and clothes dryers. When we found ourselves short of money, she was there to auction off anything in sight, including her husband's socks and boxers.

Erma and I became such allies that our friendship took us on a Greek vacation. At a restaurant, I'll never

forget the look on her face when the waiter brought her a
stack of dishes to toss and break in the custom of the
country. With each shattering sound, Erma cast her eyes
toward heaven and exclaimed, "God forgive me."

Erma was a practicing friend. I had written a piece
for *Texas Monthly* called "The Silver Lining," which I
sent to her. She called to say, "That's a book, Liz. I'm
calling my agent, Aaron Priest." In two days, he was in
Austin demanding an outline, and in another month he
had auctioned the book for the most money I ever made
at one time.

The last I saw of her, she had invited me to Phoenix
to speak at a luncheon to raise money for her favorite
cause, the Arizona Kidney Foundation. She came to the
event, despite her growing health problems. When she
walked in with her mother, her husband, and her family,
the room of more than 1,000 people stood and cheered.

The last few years, Erma has kept laughing and writing, despite a run of bad luck: a mastectomy that prevented her from getting a kidney several years ago, a fall on her shoulder recently, and the long wait for the phone call telling her that a kidney was available. For someone who gave so much laughter, it doesn't seem fair that so many bad things could happen to a person who was so kind and good.

Erma was with me a few days after I became a substitute mother at 71. She looked at me in astonishment and said, "Liz, don't you know teenagers are hazardous to your health? If it is adventure you want, why don't you go to Mount Rushmore, attach a bungee cord to Lincoln's wart, and jump?"

That's the way she faced whatever life handed her, and I suspect, knowing her deep faith in God, she is at peace with this Last Great Adventure.

Farewell, my friend.

Eulogies should give the flavor of the person. Don't give a résumé—they've already read that in the obituary. A eulogy doesn't have to be long, but it should bring memories that uplift the grieving. It should speak a message of love to the family. It should impart in a very personal way how much the listeners meant to the deceased.

Two of my closest friends were Alma Jeane Ward and her husband, Fred Ward. They were part of our seniors network singing group, the G-BATTs ("Getting Better All the Time"), for which Alma Jeane nimbly played piano. They died within a couple of years of each other.

When I was asked to eulogize Alma Jeane, it was the softness of her spirit and manner that came to mind.

ALMA JEANE WARD
Austin, Texas, July 28, 1995

Alma Jeane Ward had a flair, a style that was distinctly hers. And she had Fred, the darling of her life, and all the rest of you darlings, her children and grandchildren. You gave her great happiness, and she spread it around.

I will always remember her as being so soft — a wisp of chiffon scarf floating about her, a gown with a handkerchief skirt that moved gently as she walked, sometimes a hat framing that lovely face with the sparkling eyes that smiled and laughed and believed in you, a belief that encircled the whole world.

Her faith in humankind was whole and eternal. She saw things so clearly, right to the point. She knew who she was and how she fit into God's universe.

Yet, with all her softness, she gave strength to all of us. And I say to her family — Fred and Cristen and Shannon and the rest — you gave her the precious final gift: you walked her into heaven in the comfort of your arms.

Later, Fred passed away and, once again, I was asked to deliver the eulogy.

FRED WARD
Austin, Texas, September 15, 1997

The bow tie was his trademark. So were his smile and his loving heart. They were constants in his life and in ours.

None of us who sang with Fred will forget him. For one thing, he was always on time—and on key— at rehearsals. He was our fashion plate, even at 85. He dressed better than anyone else—a tweed vest and the latest in slacks and jackets, and when we commented on his attire, he always would credit his daughters for picking it out.

We could count on him. He could write words to songs. And he could dance soft-shoe with a jaunty straw hat and a cane, like the vaudeville stars of his youth.

Fred never was one to sit on the sidelines. He wanted to be part of the scene, to be involved. I think of an evening in 1990 when we were entertaining at a fundraiser for Ann Richards. Lily Tomlin was there watching his solo number, wide-eyed as he danced until he literally dropped. His heart had stopped. All of our hearts stopped. But your grandmother kneeled down, took his hand, and called him back, "Fred, come back. I need you." And he began breathing again.

Now he has moved on to the wider stage to join Alma Jeane—because he needs her. He has not liked being without her.

———————— ▪╪╪▪ ————————

Eulogies for family members tug at your heart because you know them so well. Yet, that is the very reason you should rise to the occasion. When my only sister and my two brothers died, I was needed and postponed the tears for a while.

———————— ▪╪╪▪ ————————

ALICE SUTHERLAND ROMBERG
Gonzales, Texas, July 1978

Friends and family of Alice and John—
In the corner of an old cemetery, in a cloister of

holly trees, I once came upon a famous statue — a shrouded figure looking into the future, emotionless. People call it "grief," but the artist, reflecting the deep passion of loss, called it "beyond all pain and joy."

These past years, we have seen Alice — once so full of laughter and energy during John's lifetime — suffer deep grief and emptiness.

This service today is a renewal of life for her — the release from her sadness on earth to the Heavenly Father, where she can be, once more, happy and at home with John.

Our faith that this is so makes the parting bearable.

As we reconcile our emotions here with her happiness beyond, we remember times before when they were together, and life was full and good.

Will you indulge our family as we live a moment in the memory of those days?

It was 1939. Alice fell in love with a man . . . and a town . . . and his family took ours as part of theirs. Quiet, patient, and orderly, John seemed to delight in the spirited, talkative, impromptu Sutherlands.

Some in this room remember the week before the wedding when our rambling old house in Austin — always full of coming and going, never locked, the house where my mother and father had moved us to see their children through "The University" — was filled with great readying and excitement. Everyone joined in the gigantic house-cleaning for the reception. (For we were a family of books more than brooms.)

With mop, dust cloth, and sweeper, we stormed the downstairs, stopping as we came upon lost treasures: two spoons under a cushion in the couch, a few coins and, yes, behold, the family butcher knife, missing for months from the kitchen!

Even the pictures on the living room wall got a going-over. Behind the glass, we found one painting was not the foggy scene of an old river in France, painted in the misty manner of Monet, as we always had thought, but a clear castle on a hill. We laughed and debated whether we had improved it.

The day came, and down the aisle came the oldest niece—four years old, a flower girl. I was maid of honor.

And then they were gone to Gonzales. "Big G," she called it with affection. In letters to us, she romanticized the people of this county to us, all the goings-on: the elections, the life at the courthouse, that wonderful old courthouse that marked their lives and ours as we came to know where government is close—valid, real, people.

After the death of our mother and father, who are buried here, John and Alice's home and shaded yard on Qualls Street was the family gathering place, our crossroads for holiday feasts.

The cars would pull up early, and children piled out, racing to the washtub of iced-down Cokes under an oak tree, more Cokes than they had seen before. There was a bountiful table, and afterward, we settled down to good talk, debate and tales, embellished in the telling.

John and Alice never had children, yet they had dozens of them by blood and affection. We added them up yesterday: 23 nieces and 2 nephews, 19 grandnieces and nephews, Sutherlands and Rombergs. Many are here today—the flower girl, now grown and a mother of three.

Two nieces were married before their fireplace, with John conducting the ceremony. Two grandnieces are Alice's namesakes. I entrusted my own two children to them for three months, and they loved going to school here in Gonzales.

There were other children, too, drawn by affection. The whole neighborhood was in and out. And bringing dogs and cats, known and unknown, to be buried under a grove of lavender trees, with appropriate rites. Every milestone was a special event.

"They make us feel young," Alice once said.

So, here we are, knowing their gift was the finest one of all—a gift of self, giving us a sense of family and joy in getting together. We remember all that today and for all our lives.

Our oldest brother sums up its meaning: "In a time of confused and changing superficiality, this couple supported each other with a clear understanding of what is right, and in death, their spirit and values live within us and fortify our embattled souls, as if to tell us the love of one another is a sign of the infinite, the measureless, ultimate truth."

We take with us today that talisman of Alice and John.

THOMAS SHELTON SUTHERLAND IV
Austin, Texas, September 1992

A true son of the West, Thomas Shelton Sutherland loved horses, knives, guns, and women, and he had them all for most of his life. He spoke Spanish with a lyrical love for the whole culture, and he taught it, as well as the literature of the Southwest. He traveled Mexico, hitchhiking as a teenager, and he became the first executive director of the Texas Good Neighbor Commission, where he fought for equality.

He was a storyteller to his family and his students, telling with gusto all that he had absorbed by growing up in Bell County, graduating with an M.A. from the University of Texas and the University of Mexico. He learned from "the trial fields of life," which he considered the best of all experiences. Everyone interested him—his children, his grandchildren, or a clerk at Wal-Mart.

Now for some personal observations because a sister can say this:

Tommy Sutherland was the most loving, hilarious, and exasperating man I have ever known. First, a word on exasperation.

His head was full of poetry, philosophy, the great works of Mark Twain and William Shakespeare—sometimes to a fault to those of us who are compulsive about organization. He could overlook the ordinary rules of life, like tidiness and structure, and even the most basic necessities of living.

Once, when I dropped by his house, he was reading—for the umpteenth time—*Huckleberry Finn*. He was reading by a dilapidated old lamp. The globe had burned out, and Tommy had taped a flashlight onto the shade with heavy silver tape. That was the light he was using. I was disgusted and said so: "Why don't you buy a light bulb? What are you going to do when the flashlight burns out?"

He grinned and said, "I'll just tape on a jar of lightning bugs."

That was the way he lived, keeping his mind on the larger picture, a picture always of hope and love and human happiness, instead of coping with the mundane things of life—like electricity.

Only Tommy could bring together in this room two former wives, ten children from two families, most of his sixteen grandchildren, three stepchildren, and innumerable cousins—talkative Sutherlands, proud Robertsons, friends who spend their life arguing—and expect it to work.

But maybe it can work. And that's where the loving and the high heart and the laughter come in.

For me and for my brothers, George and Bill, we have lost our beloved oldest brother. And I have lost my steady supplier of Bartlett's Quotations—my wordsmith who always could remember, even at 5:30 in the morning, the line from Browning or Tennyson that our mother used for appropriate situations. I would phone him and read him my copy for a magazine piece or a chapter of a book, and he would give me a better word in a key part that made all the difference.

Tommy had that rare capacity to rise above the mundane in the midst of disaster and turmoil. I never saw him lose heart or faith.

It is a great solace to his family that he will be buried among his ancestors and friends in the State Cemetery. A great-great-grandfather, the impresario Sterling C. Robertson, and William Menefee, a great-great-uncle — both signers of the Texas Declaration of Independence — are buried here.

Nearby, he has friends and fellow Texas storytellers: Fred Gipson, Walter Prescott Webb, J. Frank Dobie.

I find a sense of peace and continuity there under that grove of trees, as you will. And because I know something about life and death, I promise all of you that our association with his loving spirit is not over. In the years ahead, his memory will give us laughter, words, and counsel when we least expect it, for he loved us all.

———————— ◆◆ ————————

GEORGE ROBERTSON SUTHERLAND
Austin, Texas, November 5, 1997

Everybody needs a brother like George. Or a husband, a father, a grandfather like "Papa George," an uncle or cousin or a friend like George. He was all of these, in this circle of friends and family.

Telephoning across the country to track us all down during the last 36 hours, I have heard the words that mean "George."

"Steadfast." "The rock in the family." "Our anchor." "Stalwart." "Loyal." "Fair." "Good." That word cropped up a lot. Just plain, unvarnished "GOOD."

≫111≪

His children think of George as always there with "unconditional love." Jean thinks of that line in the Austin High song: "faithful and true-hearted."

"He liked everyone—some more than others," Jean said.

"Valiant," Cactus said, "and a listener. I loved having him in the audience."

Then, over the dinner table, came a word that really fits—from a younger family member: "George is permanent. We could find him."

Mary learned that when she broke her arm at school, and it was George who got there to get it set. Permanent.

Isn't that what we all seek in this too-busy, fast-moving, fast-changing world? Something permanent, fixed in our lives? Someone we can count on?

I discovered that 50 years ago when I first went to Washington to look for a job and ran out of money. Frantically, I wired George in Lubbock: "If you don't send me $200, I am going to have to sell my body to the Smithsonian." He wired right back: "Sell it by the pound!" But he sent the $200.

Now, I have to tell you, especially you grandchildren, what it was like to be little kids together. We were just two and a half years apart, so I have known George since before he could walk or talk. He was crazy about tomatoes. I still can hear him at the dinner table, saying, "More 'maters." He said it a lot.

In the Salado summertimes, at our grandmother's house in the country, we were playmates—inseparable. We would play house around the gnarled roots of a big live oak tree, outlining the rooms between with pebbles. Dressing acorn people with their little hats. Or we would play "store" with the "Money Tree"—a large ash tree behind the kitchen that dropped flat, dime-sized pods. We bought and sold groceries with those pods.

Some days, our Uncle Sterling would lift us up

on the tamest (and slowest) mare, Betty, and we would ride double down to the post office at Norwood's Store. Sometimes we would stop and crawl into the spooky cave under the Stagecoach Inn, cooled by the spring waters. We could stir up some excitement by poking at the thousands—no millions—of daddy longlegs clinging to the ceiling. You have no idea how exciting that can be—all those daddy longlegs scuttling all over the place. It was an enchanted childhood—freedom to roam the pastures, with a horse as a babysitter.

That was before the mad dog got us both, and we came down to the Pasteur Institute to have 21 shots in the stomach. To show you how forgiving he was, George never stopped liking dogs. He always had a dog, and he understood them and how to listen to them. I can ignore dogs.

In 1928, like so many Texas families, when the oldest child, Tommy, was ready for the University, my mother moved us to Austin to get educated. Austin— our Athens on the hill, O. Henry's "City of the Violet Crown."

When George graduated into Austin High School, he found the love of his life, Jean Taber, sitting beside him on the first day in his homeroom class. She told me about it: "We sat alphabetically, so the SUs were next to the TAs." Yes, there was Jean—never anyone but Jean. Those two were the best jitterbuggers at high school dances, and they did a memorable performance at their Golden Wedding Anniversary party. I never can hear "In the Mood" or "Mack the Knife" without thinking of them.

Some of you here, like Johnny Lucius and Cactus Pryor, knew George when he was a tackle on the football team—number 40, under Coach Staudard Lambert. Or some of you, like Travis Raven, knew George when he went out for track, and his sweetheart became the Track Team Sweetheart.

Jean and George—the undaunted team of half a century. All of us turned to them to draw strength from that loving and sturdy partnership.

A wise woman, Lady Bird Johnson, once told me: "Remember, love never ceases to be." You are going to find that true, Jean.

It is great to see so many Sutherlands here from Uvalde and Boerne, from Scott's Bluff, Nebraska, and from San Francisco. George's family—and what a tribute they are to their parents—is always there.

In the family circle, George was the one we turned to automatically for the blessing or the benediction. He leaves us both blessing and benediction, a gift he gave us by example: Be there for each other.

I got quite a start yesterday when I called his house and heard his voice still on the recording: "Hello . . . (hesitating)," and then, "We're not here right now, but we want to talk to you."

He always will be there for us—guiding us, speaking to us in our prayers and in our thoughts. Yes, George is permanent in each of us.

Only recently, I eulogized my close friend and neighbor, Emmett Shelton, the late great developer of Westlake Hills in Austin. Although all Emmett's friends and family were saddened by his departure, we could not reasonably lament his death, as he lived to the ripe age of 95. Instead, I talked about Emmett's accomplishments in the great expanse of his life—and his love of the hillside enclave that he founded and fashioned into a breathtaking retreat that I call home to this day.

EMMETT SHELTON
Austin, Texas, March 21, 2000

Old Austin and New Austin—he loved them both
and lived them fully. Imagine, 95 years—a near-century he
lived in this town, now a city. He saw it grow from 25,000
to nearly a million. Relished it, from the time the first air-
plane flew over Austin when he crawled up on the roof of
the Shelton cottage on West Live Oak in South Austin and
waved to the pilot.

Years later, he was lured to the hills west of Austin,
and he became the nurturer of a growing village. He collected not only land and arrowheads, but also tales of the
moonshiners and cedar choppers who lived there and paid
him in land to get them out of trouble. He collected the
folklore of life, as he knew it, and he shared. Yes, thanks
to his foresight, you can find it in the Austin History
Center and the archives of Southwest Texas State University and the University of Texas Law School, where
the folklore can never be erased by time.

When he was 90, he celebrated with a party, and the
G-BATTs (our senior group) wrote a song for him. The
tune is familiar—let it run through your mind, as I read:

> *We've grown accustomed to your face,*
> *It's been around for 90 years.*
> *We've grown accustomed to your smile*
> *Preserving, Westlake style,*
> *Your bugle blast, your lively past.*
> *You are a lawyer who could win,*
> *No matter what your client's sin.*
> *You are a poet and a lover,*
> *Wrote some books and published, too,*
> *You bridged the Colorado*
> *And you opened Westlake's view.*

We've grown accustomed to your yarns
Of Austin's many charms . . .
Accustomed to your face.

My home is just across the road from Emmett's last home on Skyline Drive. Once, we were having an old-fashioned stump-speaking at my house. Emmett and a helper arrived, dragging a giant tree stump which still rests in my front yard. Emmett had rescued it during a land-clearing, and he wanted me to have it, so he told me its story.

The old tree stump once was a majestic cypress that grew in Westlake Hills. It had withstood wind and sun,

lightning, storms and drought, but its seedlings took root around it to make the hills more beautiful.

"If this old tree could speak," Emmett said, "it could tell you of Indians and even buffalo who lived in these hills. It is nature's way of balancing people and land. Now its branches are gone and its roots disintegrated to replenish the soil. Even in death, the old tree speaks to us and reveals the wonder of God's creation."

Prophet, patriot, poet—Emmett, the trial lawyer for cedar choppers and moonshiners, knew and felt the beauty of the hills, and he wanted to retain it. So, he named the winding roads and tucked-away places as they should be: Red Bud Trail, Wild Cat Hollow, Old Wagon Road, Yaupon Valley Road, Liveoak Ridge, Mulberry Lane, Windsong Trail.

Like that old tree stump, the witness of so much history, even in death he continues to speak to us, and always will.

———————— ➤✦✦◄ ————————

This chapter on eulogies would not be complete without including my eulogy to Bella Abzug, the first person to be elected to Congress on a platform of women's rights and peace and a member of that group of 271 who jump-started the contemporary women's movement.

Born July 24, 1920, Bella Abzug worked as a peace activist, labor lawyer, lecturer, news commentator, civil liberties advocate, and United States congresswoman. She cofounded the National Women's Political Caucus and coauthored the Freedom of Information and Privacy acts, which restricted the FBI's right to withhold information from the public. Bella was a real hero for women in the United States: While serving in Congress, she cast one of the first votes for the Equal Rights Amendment, and she was a tireless worker for women's and minorities' rights, disarmament, and safeguarding the environment. She was one of the most vocal supporters for U.S. withdrawal from Vietnam in the '70s, and she was the first member of Congress to call for President Nixon's impeachment.

Bella's trademark wide-brimmed hats and decidedly blunt speech helped to enshrine her as an icon of the strong, resourceful American woman.

BELLA ABZUG
New York City, New York, April 1998

Bella was a mixture of brass and velvet. She gave force and love. Life for women is better because of her. We couldn't have done it without her, and I always will be grateful that I saw her in action for a quarter of a century.

We met on Capitol Hill in May of 1971. I was fresh from the Johnson White House, and so many were surprised to see me there, as Bella and many of them were anti-Vietnam, anti-LBJ. But I was raised a feminist, and LBJ was supportive of women's appointments and causes. I wanted to show up for him, as well as for me and my daughter, Christy.

In the weeks and years ahead, we met frequently in committees and conventions, and we came to appreciate each other—all of us. So much is owed to that catalyst group of 271 founders. Bella kept us moving.

The moment I will always cherish was watching Bella and Martin Abzug being interviewed on TV. The interviewer, obviously in awe of Bella, asked Martin how he could be married to someone so fiery and, well, pushy.

"GREAT SEX!" was Martin's instant reply.

Martin adored her. He worried about her, but he was 100 percent for all she was doing. Whenever she spoke of her daughters and Martin, her voice softened.

She believed in love and, to my surprise, was one of the first to call me the morning after my husband's death. Her voice was full of compassion, and it enveloped me with sympathy. I will never forget.

It surprised me at the time, for I had known her best in the heated moments of those noisy organizing days of the National Women's Political Caucus. I remember seeing her in the Caucus Room of the House Office Building one morning when we first met to lay the groundwork for the national caucus. She was cheery, urging everyone to have some coffee and doughnuts. She could be hospitable and tough, full of fury and, on occasion, full of laughter. But that was what it took. Her strength stiffened our resolve.

Today, I rub my eyes in wonder that so much has happened since those early days, but it should have happened, and it would not have happened without Bella.

It is great to see the growing number of women in Congress and in state legislatures, and to see a secretary of state who knows how to bring about peace. After years of viewing television newscasts of that all-male group in Brooks Brothers suits not getting anywhere at the various peace talks, we now see the short-skirted, stylish Madeleine Albright, with jangling bracelets, walking confidently with two Middle Eastern leaders on either side. She knows how to make foreign policy make sense to people. It will take women—lots of us—to make peace on Earth.

Thank God for Bella.

I resent the image that Texas is "bubba-land." We have our bubbas, but we also have women who know a bubba for what he is.

— L. C.

9

WELCOME TO TEXAS

I have served as the captain of the Welcome Wagon for groups visiting Texas numerous times. Those always are interesting occasions because virtually everyone who comes to Texas for the first time has some preconceived notion about our state, and often that notion is patently false. The misconceptions can be pretty wild, as my fellow Texans will attest, and they almost always equate Texas with unbridled bragging. Fittingly, then, the speech that I've included in this section is called my "Bragging on Texas" speech.

Whether you're welcoming people to Texas, New York City, or Podunk, you have the same requirements. You've got to introduce your city in a warm and inviting way, and you've got to do it in a hurry: Most welcoming remarks are brief, lasting only two to five minutes, unless you are asked for a 30-minute brag.

Don't highlight the area's main attractions—everyone knows about them. Skim over the obvious charms that everyone expects you to herald, and exaggerate the heck out of the little-known ones. Your words must inspire the listener to want to get out and roam the place as soon as you stop talking.

The first speech I'll share with you is the one I used to welcome a diverse group of women who all had one thing in common—they were new residents of the city of Austin.

WOMEN'S NEWCOMERS CLUB OF AUSTIN
Austin, Texas, April 14, 1994

Welcome to Texas! Whether you arrive in Texas by birth, horseback, wagon train, jetliner, auto, or UFO, Texas is the kind of state that lets you belong to it. Before you know it, you have taken on our native habits of embellishing stories (there's no law against it), enjoying our characters (and becoming one), exercising our sense of loyalty (which seems to have disappeared from everywhere else), and practicing optimism (Texas is my kingdom!). Have you ever known any other state that could claim such a pattern of optimism?

I have witnessed a lot of Texas history, known a lot of Texas heroes and some of its scoundrels, and like many daughters and great-great-granddaughters of pioneer Texas, I have thrilled to the wondrous variety that is Texas. My people came here in 1829, long before the words "feminism," "networking," and "choice" were part of the female dictionary. There certainly were bossy, pushy women then, but Texas wouldn't have made it without them.

I resent the image that Texas is "bubba-land." We have our bubbas, but we also have women who know a bubba for what he is. As Ann Richards once defined him, "Bubba is the kind of guy who spends his time doing nothing in particular except kicking rocks around."

Throughout history, we have had men who are totally supportive of women. From the fall of the Alamo to the Great Depression to Chapter 11, our frontier faith remains steadfast.

It is engrained in our history: the Alamo fell, but there was Houston and San Jacinto; if the tornado knocked down the oil rig, neighbors came to help you upright it; and if the cattle stampeded in a blizzard, Little Joe the Wrangler would ride out and turn the herd. We firmly believe, as a state and as individuals shaped by the blue skies and open spaces, that if today is bad, tomorrow will be better.

There are dozens of Texan expressions that say so:

- Pore — "We wuz so pore, the fleas left the dogs and went to Dallas."
- Cold — "You don't know cold until you've been in Amarillo. There's nothing between you and the North Pole but a barbed wire fence, and it only has two strands."

During the Great Depression and the recession of the '80s — I have been through them both, and I never heard a whiner — I have heard and seen amazing things. I heard a cowboy say, "Well, hell, I can get along without a plane. I still have a hoss or two." I have seen a politician hold a garage sale — on TV. We ignore the fact that Texas, which in its early rough-and-tough days was a place that had every reason to fail, remains a success.

You have your license now. Go forth and be a Texan!

––––––––––– ➡️╫ ╫⬅️ –––––––––––

Within the last few years, to the great surprise of Austin's Chamber of Commerce, planeloads of city fathers and mothers from across the country have come to town to study our city's success story. They were flabbergasted when a group of San Franciscans showed up. For the occasion, I was asked to do a full repertoire on the

virtues of Austin over San Francisco. As with any
informed speech, I did some research.

I call this my "Bragging on Texas" speech.

SAN FRANCISCO CHAMBER OF COMMERCE
Austin, Texas, October 13, 1999

Friends from San Francisco—
Welcome to Austin! I come here a sixth-generation
Texas artifact, a liberal Democrat—one of the few who
claims it—an aging feminist and one who has, at 79 years
of age, witnessed a lot of Texas history, known a lot of
its heroes and some of its scoundrels.

If I may speak for all of Austin—well, let's make
that all of Texas—we are flattered, really flattered, that
even before San Francisco won *Money Magazine*'s "Miss
Livability" contest, you wanted to come pick up some
pointers from us—sweltering, drought-ridden Austin.
Then, when you took *Money*'s top honors, I thought
surely you would cancel. But here we are tonight, almost
on the brink of the millennium, poised to share secrets.

I have been boning up. I checked out the 1936 version of MGM's *San Francisco*, with Jeanette MacDonald,
Clark Gable, and Spencer Tracy. I wanted to confirm what
I remembered—that the song actually does say, "San
Francisco, open your Golden Gate, don't let *no* stranger
wait"—a double negative worthy of Dan Quayle. The
error was corrected in later sheet music: "Don't let *a*
stranger wait," but that's not the way it was written. We
had a governor down here who liked to quote the Bible.
He would say, "Remember, man does not live by bread
ONLY." He was defeated.

Of course, I know San Francisco has a corner on great
city songs. We all love "I Left My Heart in San Francisco,"

and I am told by real insiders that it also could be "I Left the Entire Contents of My Wallet in San Francisco."

Yes, I reviewed the pointers of both San Francisco and Austin to see how we would fare. We have no Sharon Stone, but we have Sandra Bullock. We have no Robin Williams or *Beach Blanket Babylon,* but we do have Cactus Pryor and Esther's Follies. We have no alligators, but we have bats — lots and lots and lots of bats — which prevents us from getting into a debate over how to strengthen the bridges. Austin is wild about endangered species, and topping that list are the millions of bats that sleep under the Congress Avenue Bridge. Two good restaurants feast on them — not literally, but they draw customers who want to see the bats take flight each night between 7:40 and 8:40.

You have "Da Mayor." We can't compete with that. All we have is "A Mayor." In fact, your "Da Mayor" is a Texan. He was born in Mineola, Texas, the railroad town from which the late and great House Speaker Sam Rayburn first embarked for Washington, D.C. I know there are days you would like to send him back to us, and we could use him.

Actually, in the current political situation, we could use Walter Schorenstein, too. Every cotton-picking state official, including every member of the Texas Supreme Court, is a Republican. I rub my eyes in wonder. I grew up in the Bible Belt of Democratic Texas. I was 16 before I saw my first Roman Catholic and 21 before I met my first Republican. Both were terrifying experiences. We were Methodist and Baptist. We knew Episcopalians for what they really are: Neiman-Marcus Methodists. We ate soul food before it was chic, and we went to prayer meetings before it was a political statement.

We still exercise loyalty (which has disappeared in many places). We still practice optimism, as we always have, from the fall of the Alamo through the Depression of the '30s through Chapter 11 in the '80s. It is ingrained in our history. Our frontier faith remains strong.

The Alamo was falling, but when Colonel Travis sent out his immortal letter, "To all Americans and Texans everywhere: We are besieged by thousands, but our fort still stands, etc.," well, 32 came. The rest is history. The Alamo did fall, but there was Sam Houston waiting to rally Texans to follow him to San Jacinto, a battle that lasted 18 minutes. Texas won. Some say it was because General Santa Anna was mixing it up with the Yellow Rose of Texas. Since then, we have written songs to honor her.

Almost everything that has made Texas great has been high-risk: oil, cattle, timber, politics. Even the weather is high-risk. But it all draws us closer and helps us appreciate one another.

We know we need neighbors. The house in Salado where I was born, built when Texas was very young, has a strangers' bedroom, not connected to the main house, so a horseman riding through town could unsaddle his horse and find a place to sleep. Austin's neighborhoods are close and as friendly as small towns. As LBJ once said, "They know when you're sick, love you while you live, and miss you when you die."

The need for one another carries on and makes us habitually inclusive and democratic. One young banker told me, "When someone from out of state enters Austin, he might expect us to look like *Giant*, but we are set among the rolling hills, along a hike-and-bike trail with plenty of parks and Barton Springs—our fountain of youth, flowing 40,000 gallons of ice-cold water each hour. There is a Polar Bear Club of old folks who swim every day—rain or shine—in Barton Springs."

Austin has the excitement of one of the country's great universities and a power structure that is very much down-home. You can be invited to all the boards, dine at the Governor's Mansion, or drop in for the best barbecue at a country place and not have a million dollars or old family background. We have a level playing field. We also have music. Sixth Street on Saturday night is a major draw. Millionaires and Dellionaires stroll down Sixth Street among the noisy students for the multitude of sounds—jazz, country western, blues, reggae, and rap. There are dozens of bars—most notably Esther's Follies, spoofing almost anything you can think of, every Friday and Saturday night. The talented acting team for "Greater Tuna" was born at Esther's Follies. Along Sixth, there also is poetry reading and gospel singing. After all, it was a country boy from the Baptist choir in Abbott, Texas, Willie Nelson, who moved the music capital down to Austin from Nashville.

Entertainment abounds in Austin, with a symphony, opera, ballet, and the "Texas Lege," as Molly Ivins calls it.

I give a lot of credit for our state's spirit to mass smiling. I have a Yankee relative who won't come here because he gets tired of smiling. We smile a lot, and we laugh a lot, and, like your beautiful city, we have a high tolerance for colorful characters, such as the great short story writer O. Henry, who named Austin "The City of the Violet Crown." Of course, it has other names, too— including "Lady Lib City." Our first women's libber was a German-born artist, Elisabet Ney, who came here before the turn of the century and shocked Texas by riding astride, instead of sidesaddle, wearing flamboyant capes, and entertaining the brightest brains that came through Austin: Paderewski, Caruso, and the ballerina Pavlova. She entertained from her hammock, serving tea and clabber (was this the early version of yogurt?). She was the favorite dinner guest of Colonel E. M. House, the president-maker and adviser to Woodrow Wilson.

She was commissioned to do two Texas statues— Stephen F. Austin and Sam Houston—for the United States Capitol Building, as well as for our own State

Capitol Building. When critics questioned the fact that they were not the same height in life, but were in her works, she replied, "Take it up with God. He made the men, not I." Ever since, women have been talking back.

Take Ann Richards. (I wish they hadn't.) Ann described the plight of women better than anyone. "Ginger Rogers did everything Fred Astaire did. She just did it backwards and in high heels."

We Texans relish humor. When James Michener came down here to write about Texas, on the night he arrived, about six people told him he must include the famous "Sam Houston Soup Story" in his text. What is it?

Sam Houston was dining with friends, and when he tasted his soup, it was boiling hot. He spewed it out all over the guests. Dead silence followed, as they waited for him to apologize. Then he spoke: "A damned fool would have swallowed that."

Of course, the ultimate Texan of recent times — in the image of Sam Houston — was the president I knew best, Lyndon Johnson. Often, he is described as "larger than life," and he was. Even now, 30 years later, when we hold periodic LBJ reunions, everyone comes to share and rejoice in LBJ folklore. The most recent reunion was in May, when more than 500 people showed up at the LBJ Library for the love-in that binds us together. And our ties to the man who, as Bill Moyers put it, "drove like hell, could cuss like a sailor and show his gallbladder scar to the world, but who also was a man who believed poverty could be scourged, who nailed Medicare down and who held a day-long festival of the arts to which he invited everyone in the cultural world who hated him."

Bill recalled how LBJ often didn't mean what he told you to do. One evening, he had a particularly furious scrap with McGeorge Bundy, whom he thought was leaking information to the *Washington Post*.

Bill followed the president up to his bedroom late in the evening, and LBJ said, "Bill, would you mind getting my pajamas that are behind the door? Then find my robe in the other room."

"No, not at all," Bill said.

And then the president added, "Bill, when you've done that, would you go fire McGeorge Bundy?"

After he returned home in 1969, his energies were devoted to the LBJ Library, and he couldn't keep his hands off of the plans. At the last minute, LBJ flabbergasted the architect, Gordon Bunshaft, by adding the replica of the President's Oval Office to the blueprints. It had to be whittled down to $7/8$ size and shoehorned in.

Harry Middleton, the director, tells about walking with the president through the library a few days before it opened in 1971. The exhibits had been designed to show the accomplishments of the Johnson years. LBJ thought something was missing.

"I don't want another damned credibility gap," he said. "That was a controversial period, and I got some pretty mean letters. The exhibits ought to show that. Let's find the meanest letter we ever received and put it in there." Archivists were dispatched to look through the files for "mean letters," but nothing satisfied LBJ. One afternoon, he took a hand in the search himself, going through box after box, steeped in the rancor that once had hounded him. Finally, with a flourish of triumph, he produced a postcard written by a man from— of all places—Linden, California. It read: "I demand that you, as a gutless sonovabitch, resign as President of the United States."

"You can't get much meaner than that," LBJ said. And the postcard went into a newly created exhibit on controversies.

It was at this time that he cleared up the question of what the LBJ Library would offer to scholars and the public. LBJ wanted it all open—warts and all.

"Good men have been trying to save my reputation for 40 years, and not a damn one's succeeded. What makes you think you can?" he told Harry Middleton.

"I suppose," he added, "you think that if I pick up the paper one day and read about something in these files I don't like, I'll raise hell."

"The thought has occurred to me," Harry replied.

"Well, if that ever happens," LBJ said, "I want you to go out and sit on the hill in front of the library. Take a lot of deep breaths, and think of everything we've been through to get this library opened. And then you come back to your office and you call me. I'll be right here waiting for your call because I'll be expecting it. You say, 'Mr. President' — because that's the way you talk, you're always very polite — 'one of us is full of shit, and we've got to decide right now who it is.'"

So the policy of the LBJ Library was set. And so it remains today — open to all, as scholars conduct their endless search to find the essential LBJ. I am so glad you will be there and that you also will see the Lady Bird Johnson National Wildflower Center. They serve as evidence, along with our series of lakes and dams, of the lasting impact we have from those two people. Thanks to Lady Bird's love of wildflowers and her influence on putting the environment and beauty of the landscape on the national agenda, wildflowers have become a money crop in Texas. They are a major tourist attraction in spring and fall, bringing hundreds of tours at wildflower time.

Now I think I have told you everything about Austin. One more important item: We are a city that is eager to hang on to its open heart and creative soul. While some cities worry about failure, we worry about success. Could all these newcomers — the engineers and computer types — change our laid-back lifestyle of writers, songsters, scholars, and freethinkers? To our delight, the new invasion by software companies — nearly a thousand of them so far — is helping us save our creative soul.

Our favorite dropout from the University of Texas, Michael Dell, and his Dellionaires (at latest count 3,000 new millionaires) are contributing to the cultural side of the city with million-dollar contributions to the Austin Children's Museum, the Austin Art Museum, and the Jewish Center.

Today, we have a city of longtime right-brainers, joined happily by big payloads of left-brainers. It is a marriage that is going to leave us living happily together for a long time — once we solve the traffic problem.

Humor is contagious, just as griping is. We all know congenital gripers. Get rid of them. I give them three gripes and they are out, out, out.

— L. C.

10

Speeches to Senior Groups: Growing Old with Grace and Humor

I always am surprised when I go into a restaurant or other establishment and people treat me with great deference. At 79, I don't see myself as old, but I'm not looking at me. My theory on how to stay young at heart is to surround yourself with a network of friends of all ages. Your children and your other relatives may scatter, but that doesn't mean you have to isolate yourself to your own age group.

Laugh. Spend every possible moment with light-hearted people. It is the cure for all that ails you, the secret to longevity. It is the key to a long, happy life that has been used by presidents and kings, rich and poor, Democrats and Republicans.

Nearly every president has had someone on their staff whose major role was to lift their spirits—someone interesting to act as a sort of court jester. Bebe Rebozo was President Nixon's practical jokester. Franklin D. Roosevelt himself was a prankster. LBJ explained his own tendency toward melancholy by saying he had too much German in him; his theory was that people of German ancestry are extremely earnest about life, so he had me to "sex up" his speeches—not to make them lascivious, but to add humor and spirit to them.

Whenever I speak to groups of senior citizens, I pepper my comments liberally with humor. Perhaps more than any other segment of the population, seniors need to laugh. And I tell them that nothing fills a life with satisfaction so much as purpose. I urge them to strike out in new directions, to pursue new endeavors—even unto the last days of their lives.

AMERICAN ASSOCIATION OF RETIRED PERSONS
San Antonio, Texas, June 2, 1992

Friends—

A speaker always wonders why he or she has been chosen to speak. For the last two years, I sometimes have thought it was because I look like Barbara Bush. I can't help it if she copied my white hair, my affinity for fake pearls, and my dress designer, Lane Bryant. Here lately, I have decided it's because I look like Texas Governor Ann Richards, only ten years older. The fact is, we all look like George Washington, so we are sought-after speakers.

Yes, the millennium came to Texas. We elected a grandmother to run this state. On behalf of Ann Richards, let me welcome you to Texas, where men are men and women are governors, railroad commissioners, chairmen of development boards, regents of universities, and mayors. There are—hold your breath—162 women mayors in Texas, in cities including Fort Worth and Corpus Christi and many small towns. And a lot of the mayors are grandmothers, too!

Present company excepted, I get some strange folks asking me to speak. My book title, *Getting Better All the Time*, confuses a lot of program chairs. There was the National Mattress Association — getting better all the time? That set them dreaming.

And there was the American Fertility Society. The president, a Dr. Buttram, called and asked me to speak, thinking mine was a medical book. (The title alone draws a lot of speech requests from doctors.) The Fertility Society was meeting in Las Vegas — a large, free-spending group of gynecologists and obstetricians.

Well, Dr. Buttram didn't read my book until the night before the meeting started and found out it wasn't medical at all, but attitudinal. So, when he introduced me, he threw his hands up in despair and said, "We are interested in women of all ages, so I give you Liz Carpenter, a post-menopausal woman." How did he know?

I can tell you, it was one of the most intimidating moments of my life. Have you ever faced 3,000 gynecologists without so much as a sheet between you?

Actually, I never thought of myself as particularly funny, but I have noticed here lately, as I walk through a room, a ripple of laughter follows me. Which is why I took time off and headed for the Pritikin Institute, where I lost 10 pounds, my memory, and my taste buds in two weeks, making my doctor happy. Mealtime — that is stretching the word — was a time when you had to laugh, for there was nothing to chew.

My text today is based on the remarkable quotation from Helen Keller, and I want you to think about it: "Life is an adventure or nothing at all."

Just think about it — that applies to every aspect of your life.

Two things will serve you well in going about the adventure of life — the adventure of living. One is a sense of humor. The other is a sense of purpose outside of your own self-interest. I want to talk about them both, and I've learned a lot more about both subjects recently.

You see, I am into unplanned parenthood. Yes, at 71 years of age, I have become a born-again mother. Last fall, I inherited two teenagers to raise. My late brother, Tom Sutherland, raised ten children in two batches. By now, seven are grandmothers and the rest just out of Play-Doh.

But anyway, I was chosen by fate and luck and default to raise these three kids. It has been eye opening. While I thought I would be the oldest person at the PTA meetings, the place is alive with surrogate parents—single fathers, single mothers, grandparents, and aunts—all struggling to do right by their children.

Raising kids is a whole new scene since my days of motherhood 30 years ago. Take music—if you can call it that. To sing along as you drive along is OUT. New metallic noises on the car radio are IN. I never realized what a blessing it is to have a hearing impairment. You need a deaf ear to turn when Slaughter and the Slayer or the Megadeth group comes on with something likely to be called, "Do it! Do it! Do it!" Lousy advice, as you know. It is tough to be a parent in today's world.

But it is also very tough to be a kid today. There are a lot of demons out there that you and I never had to face. Which is why we are needed. And God knows, one of the gratifications at my age is that this experience makes me know I am still needed, and I still have a sense of humor.

As you age—and we are all aging from the day of the first primal cry—we need humor, more and more. I find laughter more necessary as I enter the springtime of my senility.

My own particular attitude about aging is that I'm still the same person inside this silver head that I've always been. I still feel like I'm just out of the University of Texas, looking for adventure.

I'm not—as I was reminded forcefully last month

when I attended the 50th reunion of the graduating class of 1942. But I was cheered to see how many of us have done rather well for ourselves, our families, and our communities. We grew up during the Great Depression and graduated into World War II—we had a sense of purpose.

I want to keep meaningful purpose in my life and lots of laughter. I want to retain the joy of discovery, and I want to continue to work to the grave, to leave my books of wisdom for my grandchildren and all other literate Americans.

Humor is essential to wellness. Laughter recharges our entire being; every cell is activated. We come alive, and full vitality restores us physically and emotionally.

In his book *Anatomy of an Illness*, Norman Cousins describes how he fought his fatal illness with laughter. He persuaded his doctors to let him check out of the hospital and into a hotel with a lot of funny books and Groucho Marx movies and, I suspect, a laugh-along nurse. After a month, he was cured and ready to write about it.

Humor is contagious, just as griping is. We all know congenital gripers. Get rid of them. I give them three gripes and they are out, out, out.

And bores. If you can't stir them up with a few tries, give up and let them bask in their own boredom. I remember the advice that Alice Roosevelt Longworth once gave me about entertaining: "If you owe a bore a dinner, send him one."

In aging, as in politics, humor is vital.

How do you know when aging has hit you? For me, it was when President Eisenhower—or was it Nixon—named Shirley Temple Black to the United Nations. Suddenly—*Bam!* I thought: Shirley Temple? That's Little Miss Marker. That's the kid with the curls who tap-dances with Bill Robinson. And with that established, suddenly I felt, well, old—and that was several appointments ago for Shirley Temple Black.

I also knew I had lived a long time when Willard Scott began to look like General Schwarzkopf, with hair. It wasn't his own hair. It was Howard Cosell's or George Burns's hair. They share a hairpiece. You never have seen them both with hair at the same time, have you?

Dave Barry, a funny columnist, said he knew he was in the aging process when he got very concerned about his gums. "There was a time," he said, "when I could go for decades without thinking about my gums, but recently they loom larger in my mind than the greenhouse effect."

Another friend of mine, Pat Paulsen, said he solved his feelings about getting old with this philosophy of life: "The wind blew, and the crap flew, and we're all just here for a day or two."

The good news is that we live longer today than ever before. We live past our warranty and long enough to get to the parts department, which is pretty much certain, as we hit our 70s. My doctor told me, "Picture yourself like an automobile." (I chose a Rolls Royce.) "Look at it this way," he said, "you go along for years, smooth riding, no skids, then suddenly a part goes out, a kneecap here, a bosom there, ears, teeth."

These things used to shelve us, but today we check in and out of the repair department and we're ready to take on the world again.

Of course, there is one part that starts going, for which there is no repair: memory.

You may have noticed that you tend to forget things. You'll be talking to someone at a party, and you'll know you know this person, but you can't remember his or her name. This can be very embarrassing, especially if he or she turns out to be your spouse.

Two women who were very good friends were having lunch and, suddenly, one of them said, "Forgive me, my dear, I know we have been close friends for years, but for the moment, I can't think of your name." The friend paused and replied, "Give me ten minutes, and I'll try to come up with it."

I had a comparable experience earlier this year. For several years now, I have been practicing the give-for-good-luck policy. Every time I get one of those envelopes soliciting money to prevent some awful disease, I pick out the ones that I am most likely to get—cancer, heart, kidneys, stomach worms—and send them a small check. I figure that if I give, God will protect me from that particular ailment.

The other day there arrived in the mail (this is a true story) a letter from the Alzheimer's Foundation. Yes, I thought, I am now in that "Big A" age bracket—so I got my checkbook, sat down, and opened the envelope. When I looked at the solicitation more closely, behold! It was a receipt and a letter thanking me for the $15 I had sent two weeks before.

Now, I don't want you to leave this occasion with just a memory of brilliant wit and high humor. That's all good fun, but we need some meat, so that we can have a clear conscience.

I told you I wanted to talk to you about two things. The first was a sense of humor. The second is a sense of purpose—and let's talk about that.

Keep doing something outside yourself, whether it is working with a hospice, saving our environment, or working for a woman candidate for public office—or running for public office yourself.

Statistically, our age group is the one most likely to vote—so let's talk about what's lacking on the public agenda where you might apply your efforts: peace, ethics and election reform, health care, education, for openers.

It doesn't take a crystal ball to see the challenges of the '90s. They are all about us, and it is a signal to people like yourselves, who are experienced in the art of creative help on so many fronts, to expand and widen your efforts. There is adventure in that!

"Change is not our enemy," President Johnson said. "On the contrary, society has no deadlier enemy than the refusal to change."

We have only to turn on a TV or read a newspaper to know that things are not working well, that our inner structures often decline to the lowest common denominator, that we seem to have lost our sense of responsibility.

The media is unfocused. As a former reporter, I am conscious that we have lost all sense of what is news. News is overwhelmingly rock stars and political scandals. And yet we know they are a small minority in America and do not deserve the space they occupy in this troubled world.

Corporate America has betrayed us on many fronts. Government responses are too slow and often hedged.

As hard as teachers try — and they do try, as do a remarkable number of volunteers and mentors who strive to make public education work — we still fall short of the needs. The homeless, the poor, the sick, the ignorant seem to be growing by leaps and bounds.

The aging population — if rallied — could help provide wise answers and a lot of volunteer support for current problems.

Like van Gogh, I believe we were not put here to be "simply happy" or "merely honest." I believe we were put here to realize great things for humanity.

Women are going to be a big part of the future. We are blessed with longer life spans in which to do the things we really want to do. There is no need for anyone to become old from a simple lack of useful work. If more people acted on this premise, the problem of discrimination against the aged would diminish greatly.

Now, I am going to close with some research and advice from a sister, aging expert and friend, Ann Firor Scott. She was inspired by reading an exchange of letters between two familiar names — Elizabeth Cady Stanton and her close friend, Susan B. Anthony. Elizabeth Stanton had just given birth to her sixth child, and Susan B. Anthony, who was single, complained about the way numerous babies were delaying their mothers' work for suffrage.

"Courage, Susan," Elizabeth wrote. "We shall not reach our prime before fifty, and then we shall have twenty good years at least."

Her expectation was too modest. They lived to be 82 and 83, respectively, each working to the last day of her life.

Like Tennyson's Ulysses, we know it is dull to pause to make an end. To rust unburnished, not to shine in use "as if to breathe were life."

And so Ulysses called his friends, his shipmates, to a cooperative endeavor:

"'Tis not too late to seek a newer world; push off, and sitting well in order to smite the sounding furrows."

Perhaps if we, too, can push off, ever in new directions, the future will be writing that the last decade of the 20th century in the United States of America developed a new élan—not in spite of, but because of its aging population.

Someone once said, "History is just one damned thing after another," but we know better than that. History is us, you and me, and the events of our times.
                                                    —L. C.

11

COMMENCEMENT SPEECHES

Why is it that an invitation to give a commencement speech causes panic? Because we feel responsibility for giving great advice to send graduates on their way into the wide, wide world. But you are kidding yourself if you think they are going to remember your immortal words. The only thing on their minds is to get it over, get out, and get to the overnight party as fast as possible.

Still, you have to say *something*, and the parents will be listening.

It's good advice to interview some of the graduates before you start writing. What do they expect?

You also should read other commencement speeches—maybe the text of last year's remarks. Maybe reading the speech I wrote for a college graduation from my own alma mater and another delivered to high school students will offer up some ideas.

Beware: High school and college students are the toughest audiences you'll ever find. Raised in the electronic age, these young people have spent a good deal of their lives being entertained by a television set—a piece of furniture that isn't interactive and doesn't require a laugh for motivation. Many a speaker has taken the microphone with an air of confidence, only to find that his witticisms drop like a rock on a hall of seemingly deaf ears. Instead of laughter, he is met with blank stares and icy silence. And *nothing* strikes fear into the heart of a speaker more than silence.

So, I often start my commencement speeches by baring my soul to the students about the trepidation with which we speechmakers approach them, and I have met with a good bit of success.

THE UNIVERSITY OF TEXAS — COLLEGE OF COMMUNICATION
Austin, Texas, December 6, 1998

Dean Wartella, friends, and families, and, most important of all, graduates —

Being asked to make a commencement speech causes panic. Can I say anything you will remember?

Russell Baker, the columnist, offered this advice to graduates about to go out into the real world: "Don't go! There's nothing but problems out there. Tell your folks you want them to shell out for another year."

I can't endorse that advice, though, because you are needed NOW. You graduates are needed to make the information explosion more than games and a litany of facts that are of no use to anyone.

If you delay, you might end up like the fellow who didn't want to get out of bed for school. His mother stood over him, berating: "If you don't get up this minute, you'll be late for school!"

"But I don't want to go to school," he said. "They

make fun of my clothes. They laugh at me in the halls. Sometimes, they throw things at me. Give me one good reason why I should get up and go to school."

"I will give you two," she replied. "You are forty years old, and you're the principal."

I come here an aging journalist, at home on this campus and with you, for it was 56 years ago that I graduated. I still have the program of that ceremony. It is bound in cowhide for all UT graduates of 1942, including the 48 of us who received our bachelor of journalism degrees.

We graduated with words as our tools and the training to use them. We were wide-eyed romantics eager to be great reporters.

If we old grads seem overly sentimental, it is because this thriving, friendly, remarkable university shaped us, both professionally and personally. It gave us a skill, a life, and a passion. Often, we met the love and partner of our lives in those classrooms. I did, and married the fellow who sat next to me in class.

Well, our old journalism school has exploded to meet the needs of a faster and wider world—a College of Communications with five departments reaching across a broad spectrum of communication and far more visual than when I graduated, when print was king. Your information highway can lead to educating the world about mankind's problems and guiding it to solutions. That's true, whether you are writing for newspapers or magazines, television or radio, film, advertising, or the Internet. It's true, also, in the thriving new field of speech disorders and better communication for those who need it most.

Indeed, so rapid are the developments in science and technology that we scarcely can know the potential of the medium with which you work.

Yes, you are needed now, and you are needed desperately. People are drowning in information, too much of which leaves them feeling cynical, frustrated, and even hopeless. What is the use of all the information if it doesn't provide answers to the world's problems?

Communication with the world is literally at our fingertips. We no longer need to research at the UT Library to get the facts. We can access them electronically in minutes. We can communicate instantaneously with people from a hundred different cultures. The world is overwhelmed and bewildered by the information explosion and badly needs your help to cut through the clutter to what is truly important.

The warning signs are out: "Information has become a form of garbage, incapable of answering the most fundamental questions," says one New York professor. "Information is dangerous when it has no place to go, when there is no higher purpose that it serves."

With facts readily available, you should be able to use them more wisely to uncover or create solutions. For example, take these two startling bits of information:

- More than a billion people in our world survive on less than $370 a year.
- Americans who constitute 5 percent of the world's population purchase 50 percent of its cocaine.

How can these problems be communicated so your audiences understand the causes and are better prepared to move toward solutions?

The information explosion must consist of more than scandal-chasing, commercial messages, and celebrity trivia.

The central questions I urge you to ask yourself are: What can we do—what can YOU do—to bring us closer to a more civilized society? How can you use your degree and new privileges of the front-row seat, the press pass, the accessibility to the powerful, for illumination and healing? Finding the answers will give your profession meaning, and meaning is what fulfillment is all about.

There are obvious differences between the challenges of your day and those of mine when I was reporting. Fifty years ago, we concentrated on getting the "five Ws and the H" — Who, What, When, Where, Why, and How. Today, a sixth "W" must be added: *What* can be done about it?

Ask yourself: How can my words, my voice, or my images provide the perspective needed to cope with the complexities of today's world?

For role models, you need to look no further than three of our own distinguished remarkable journalism alums. Walter Cronkite, Claudia "Lady Bird" Taylor Johnson, and Bill Moyers put to use the tools they gained on this campus to construct meaningful lives and careers of accomplishment for the human family. They left this campus and became — and remain — three of the most distinguished and credible living Americans. Had you been around half a century ago, you could have found their bylines in *The Daily Texan*, which, incidentally, celebrates its 100th birthday next October.

Of the three, I know Lady Bird best. My job as her press secretary was a breeze because she knew the difference between an A.M. and a P.M. The only first lady to hold a journalism degree, she asked those key questions for the reporters who covered her in the turbulent '60s.

"Maybe," she said, as we traveled this country, opening the Head Start projects, visiting the Job Corps camps, and walking the riverfronts, "maybe I can pull back the curtain a little bit wider so people will look, see, and — hopefully — act."

And she did. She underscored the difference a war on poverty, disease, and ugliness could make. She put care of the environment firmly and forever on the political agendas of mayors and presidents.

As for Bill Moyers, I was still a Washington correspondent when this very green, bespectacled young man showed up at our office in the National Press Building in Washington. We walked over to his first White House press conference—President Eisenhower's. Today, Bill is the envy of his media colleagues, who watch him create the documentaries that get right to the core of the big problems: drug addiction, campaign reform, the nature of evil. He helps us to understand Genesis, creativity, and poetry. He looks beneath the surface. He asks questions that mean something. He is not afraid to probe that unexplored world of spirituality. We are all the smarter and the more civilized for his work.

Walter Cronkite, "the most trusted man in America," is also one of our own. His 80 fabulous years from print to camera are told in his autobiography, *A Reporter's Life.* It should be *THE Reporter's Life,* for certainly it is Walter Cronkite's open mind and fair reporting, good humor, curiosity, civility, and uncompromising ethics that we envision when we think about "the ultimate reporter." On this campus, he interviewed Gertrude Stein for *The Daily Texan.* In the years that followed, he introduced us to the space age and lifted us to the stars. He helped us in our grief over a slain president, and he helped to scale down a war in Vietnam. His recollections of the city rooms of his early days ring with nostalgia. You young people may find this quaint, but maybe some of you who grew up in the days of *Front Page* or who have seen reruns of the movie will identify with it.

"I suppose," he muses, "those dedicated to most crafts take pleasure in the sights and sounds and smells peculiar to them, but I can't imagine any being as exciting as the heavy odor of printer's ink, pulp paper and melting lead, the clanking of the old Linotype machines, the deafening din of clacking news service printers, rewrite men shouting—*God, how I loved it!*"

What will happen to communications—printed and visual—in the future? We who have watched the obsession with scandal with alarm are concerned that you newcomers to our profession are entering a world that has seen a serious debasement of the journalistic principles of truth, accuracy, fairness, and a frequently ignored item—thoroughness.

Within the last 48 hours, in my own anxiety to say something that you will remember today, I turned reporter again and called all three fellow alums to ask: What should the message to communicators going into the 21st century be?

According to Walter Cronkite: "What must remain constant are the principles that must guide all serious communicators. 'Principles.' That's the key word. They will find that, as neophytes, they have little strength with which to resist employers who are all too frequently unprincipled. But, as diplomatically as possible in order to preserve their jobs, they should seek to uphold the principles and persuade management to do likewise. They should not hesitate to express their concerns and convictions in those after-hour bull sessions that are common to all offices. They will find more allies in their company than even the old-timers may have recognized."

For Lady Bird Johnson, "Journalism school began a search to learn about the wonders of the world and to pass them on. I felt that communications was a privilege I should regard with respect. I didn't want to pass out material that was tawdry, ugly, or trivial."

When I reached Bill Moyers, he was in the chaos of deadlines, but he paused long enough to say: "Journalists are licensed to explain what we don't understand, so our work is a continuing course in adult education. Never close your books—or your mind—and never presume to know what you don't know."

Think of it! These are America's standard-bearers, shaped by the same university that has shaped you.

Through the mists of half a century, the lure of this profession has remained steadfast. The same enticement that I followed 50 years ago also brought you to this college and to this day of graduation.

Like Walter Cronkite, one day you will say, "God, how I loved it."

God, how we all love it. Make it count for something, my friends. Make it count for humanity.

Invitations to speak at high school commencements generally are prompted by being kin to one of the graduates. In this case, the graduate was my niece and namesake, Liz Sutherland.

KIRBY HALL HIGH SCHOOL COMMENCEMENT
Austin, Texas, May 31, 1992

It was more than 50 years ago—shortly after the earth cooled—that I graduated from Austin High School. Our speaker was a marvelous rabbi—a round, delightful, joking man.

I can't remember a single joke. I can remember one sentence—his message to us. He looked into our eyes and right to the bottom of our bobby socks and saddle oxfords, and said firmly: "Just remember, my young friends, the so-called new morality is just a new name for the same old immorality."

I sat straight up, put my knees together tighter, adjusted my skirt, and never forgot it. Later in life, I see a lot of people who needed that speech. I find them in the headlines about bank fraud and S&L rip-offs and income tax cheaters. I hear about them on the local news: holdups or statistics about teenage pregnancies. Indeed, we seem to be surrounded in our country by people who needed to hear that rabbi.

You know and I know that they have missed out on what life is all about.

What is life all about? It's about how to move from the textbooks and the television set to the stage of life, from being a spectator to being a player. It's about being part of the action instead of just watching others be part of the action. It's about playing a part—preparing for it and doing it well, with your own flair and personal style and creativity. It's about being a giver, instead of a taker. It's knowing that learning never ends, and you must keep on finding new friends, new ideas, new truths.

I like the line from the poem: "There's a song inside of me, I can hardly wait to see what it is I have to say and the music it will play."

And you here, the graduating class of Kirby Hall, start out ahead of the game because you know about the action. You have an interested and able faculty that has tried to give you knowledge and confidence. You have caring and generous kinfolk and friends galore.

How about standing up, turning around, and giving them a hand right now!

And now, let me talk to you about being children of the world who graduate into being responsible adults of the world. Some of you have become that already, as the world's turmoil is upon you.

Right here at Kirby Hall this year, you have class-mates who already have been players in the dramatic moments of international events: an Indian girl who saw the Gulf War beginnings in Saudi Arabia, where her family lived; three Chinese boys and girls who know what it is to live in a country of impending revolution, with tanks in the streets—they found guardian angels in this country who lifted them out of it to safety and freedom.

The one I know best is Lai Laing, a remarkably talented 19-year-old pianist. He plays Chopin like Chopin and Beethoven with all the passion of Beethoven. He was there in Beijing with his friends on that dreadful day in the Square, standing before the tanks. Lai Laing already is a player. I predict that one day he will write a great symphony about that revolution. What you and I were watching on TV in wide-eyed horror was happening to some of your classmates. To Wei Liu, a pianist, and Wei He, a violinist who lived in Sichuan Province, where the streets were filled with soldiers firing on the protesters.

What happened in our town is that a University of Texas professor, William Race, helped get them out. What happened at Kirby Hall is that you took them in, gave them friendship, and helped them to learn English in record time. Families served as surrogate parents. That's the best side of our country—the reminders that there are people who are their brothers' keepers.

Lai Laing always will remember Kirby Hall: "Everyone was so nice. My classmates helped me with English words. I like them."

It thrills me to know that, in this country where we are dismayed by an atmosphere of national greed and stinginess, there are good people who step forward to make a difference in the lives of others. Maybe without even knowing it, you did.

Like the rabbi who spoke at my graduation, I have a message for you that will make life wider, bigger, more fun. The message was spoken by a remarkable woman who was born blind, deaf, and mute—Helen Keller. She overcame these handicaps with an attitude and shared her secret of life. This is it: "Life is an adventure or nothing at all."

Think about that. Practice it. Life is an adventure or nothing at all. It makes the experience of duties and dreary things more bearable. It makes the good days more exhilarating.

This year, I have been learning a lot about your age group from three teenagers who came to live with me for a while. One of them is my niece, who is here at Kirby.

I have learned that the word "like" must be used at least three times in each sentence.

I have widened my knowledge of music. I mean it. I have learned that some of it, however horrendous, is full of words about injustice and the hungry. Yes, hidden in that heavy metal sound is a message. They have taught me to listen for the words, instead of being put off by the sound.

From my 15-year-old nephew, I have learned how elastic and healthy you all are, that it is possible to watch television, talk on the phone, and dribble a soccer ball between your feet while trying to do your math problems and eat pizza. Awesome. That's real talent!

I couldn't do that, but if you can do all that, you can do anything. You can stretch yourself and your brain to provide some real help for real problems:

- To solve the problems of the homeless
- To improve the environment
- To teach conflict resolution in this troubled world.

So, let's begin, this very day, commencing on the New You—the high school graduate in transition to college and to career. Okay, what can you do tomorrow and during the next few weeks? How can you use the summer weeks ahead for your own head start to the University of Texas?

First, I prescribe a day to sleep late, really late, loll around in bed, watch TV—that's tomorrow. Then, on your feet and start on the list of things you want to do before the summer is over.

Then, widen your world of friends of different ages. Meet a seven-year-old and read to them. Have a good conversation with a 70-year-old—at least an hour. Ask them who is the person they know who takes them the farthest back in history.

Once, on a bus, I asked that of a marvelous black woman. The answer was thrilling: "I knew my great-grandmother. She lived to be 102, and she told me about watching Monticello being built." Imagine! She watched Thomas Jefferson's home being built, and that was in 1810.

Learn the names of six trees in your yard. Lady Bird Johnson taught me how much more interesting the world is if you know the names of trees and flowers and take time to smell them.

Read at least five books by five different authors.

Learn how to look for a job. For starters, learn how to speak, so you can be heard. Write a good résumé and go ask for a job, even if you have to be a volunteer. This is a political campaign year. Pick a favorite candidate and be a mail-sorter or a messenger or a newspaper clipper at their headquarters. George Bush, Bill Clinton, Ross Perot need you. Take your choice, and see what's cooking in an election in which you'll soon be voting.

Ask yourself what you are really good at doing. Ask three friends what they think you're good at doing. Cultivate that talent in college. Statistics show that you are going to change careers every five years. You are going to move six or seven times in your life.

Help someone every day. Let your friends know you care if they have a problem or heartache. You have to give friendship to get it.

Watch a sunrise and breathe in a sunset.

Stretch your spiritual side. Just before you go to sleep, spend two minutes in conversation with a Higher Power. You'll be surprised at what happens.

You are a remarkable class of 1992. Fifty years from now, when you come back for your half-century reunion, you want to be able to tell about your adventure in life and, in your heart, you want to know that you have made a difference.

The American woman has made history by playing catch-up to win the equality we missed out on when we were left out of the Constitution. In the absence of the Equal Rights Amendment, ours has been progress by a series of fits and starts.

Through it all, one of the symbolic bonds that has held women together is the quilt. In pioneer days, the quilting bee offered a place for women to gather and visit as they worked— patching, embroidering, and piecing.

Even now, in our fast-changing world, the quilt continues to be our symbol. In Dallas at the newly opened Women's Museum: An Institute for the Future, visitors are greeted by a giant electronic quilt that captures our story in a medley of fast-moving "quilt squares."

For those of us who have been part of the movement, it brings to mind the poignant words in Mary White's book, The Quilters, which I often use in speeches:

Sometimes you don't have no control over the way things go. Hail ruins the crops, or fire burns you out. And then you're just given so much to work with in a life, and you have to do the best you can with what you've got.

That's what piecing is.

The materials is passed on to you or is all you can afford to buy— your fate.

But the way you put them together is your business.

You can put them in any order you like.

—L. C.

12

THE EXPANDING WORLD OF WOMEN

When people ask me how my knee injury occurred, I tell them that I did it kicking the wall after hearing Rush Limbaugh use the term "feminazi" one more time.

Women are born leaders, with a thousand gender-inherent strengths that equip us for executive positions. Long gone in American society is the dangerous myth that so worried Betty Friedan—the idea that women should be completely satisfied with their roles as wives and mothers and that somehow it was abnormal to want a career or an identity separate from the family. Women are in positions of leadership nationwide, yet in the year 2000, on average, women still earn only 73 cents for each dollar earned by men. Yet, do women pay 73 cents on the dollar for food, health care, housing, or child care? According to the Institute for Women's Policy Research, the average 25-year-old woman who works full-time until age 65 will earn $523,000 less than the average working man.

It's painfully clear that the women's movement is not a movement whose time has passed.

Because I was there when the contemporary women's movement was founded and am one of the few originals still living, I love to tell the story over and over about that hot day in July 1971 when 271 founding women leaders from across the country met in Washington. That meeting marked the birth of the National Women's Political Caucus. I was just out of the White House, LBJ having gone back to live a more peaceful life on his ranch in Johnson City, Texas. Here is how it happened—retold 26 years later.

"THE HISTORY OF THE WOMEN'S MOVEMENT AS I KNOW IT"
National Women's Political Caucus
Nashville, Tennessee, August 4, 1995

For me, to give you women some wisdom and advice is like Mae West talking to Madonna.

Of course, I've got a million things that I would like to talk to you about: politics from 1920 to 1998; the eleven presidents I have known, some of them favorably; how it was to ride circuit for ERA when only five votes would get those last three states, cajoling, pleading with Alan Alda, Elly Peterson, Martha Griffiths and—on weekends—with Erma Bombeck.

We did everything. We auctioned off Bill Bombeck's socks and rattled Erma's rosary in the Catholic neighborhoods. We were the Thelma and Louise for ERA. We failed, but I promise you that one day it will pass, in a whisper probably, on a voice vote when Jesse Helms finally goes to that great steaming cauldron below.

I would like to talk about you and how proud we are of today's young women—our daughters, those bright young women who walked through the newly opened

doors of colleges and obtained law degrees, medical
licenses, positions on boards, and appointments by presidents. Remember, those doors didn't just swing open for
you. Someone pulled them open.

A lot of aging feminists still have broken fingernails
so that you could earn six-figure salaries, wear Donna
Karan suits, and drive Lexus cars. Now, I hear a lot about
people with jobs that are not "meaningful." The corporate
world does not always feed your eager souls. You have to
feed your own souls outside of your professions. May I
recommend that networking and community action not
only feed your souls, but they also are the most worthy
ways of helping to improve the lots of other women, children, and your country. Hang in there. Take the risks.

Remember, if you expect to find a stepping stone when you need one, you have to be one, as well.

I am an aging feminist, an artifact — and there are only a few of us left who were there the day the contemporary women's movement was born. Like the old hymn says, "I love to tell the story" of that day we moved feminism into politics, so listen carefully. You need to know your feminist roots.

It was a steamy July day in 1971. The place was the ballroom of the Statler-Hilton Hotel in Washington, D.C. We were born kicking and screaming and shouting to be heard — all 271 founders and many more who were gathered in that pulsating room. We knew something important was happening, and that something was us.

I wouldn't have missed it for anything. There were the backpack girls from Radcliffe and Stanford, fresh from the anti-Vietnam marches. They looked pretty scrubby, but they had found out that even in a peace movement, they still were the ones who were sent out for coffee and sandwiches. Someone else was calling the shots.

There were the congresswomen: Bella Abzug, with her rallying voice and marvelous hats; Shirley Chisholm, with her calm, schoolmarm manner; and Virginia Allen, the sturdy Republican woman who was willing to stick her neck out and rally more Republicans in their jacket dresses and tidy ways.

We needed them, and one of the real cruelties of history is that, when Elly Peterson, Betty Ford, and Jill Ruckelshaus brought those young Republican women into the movement — the Pat Baileys, Pat Goldmans, Bobbie Kilbergs — years later, Ronald Reagan ran them off when he dropped the ERA plank in Detroit and abandoned the fight for choice. We needed them. They were well educated, competent, and potentially fine candidates for public office.

There was the brainy Betty Friedan, whose *Feminine Mystique* fired up the women of the suburbs, leading to the formation of the National Organization for Women. There was Gloria Steinem with her long hair, aviator glasses, and miniskirt. And everyone had big handbags — tremendous, full of flying papers and documents. It's a wonder we didn't kill each other with them, but we piled them up in a corner.

Our goals were to urge women to run for office and for some of them to get elected, to pass the Equal Rights Amendment, and to organize caucuses in all the states. There were the old-line organizations like the AAUW, the League of Women Voters, and B&PW, as well as a lot of new groups like Women United, NOW, Women Upside Down, and Women Rightside Up. We were a motley group of old establishment types. Southerners like Fanny Lou Hamer and Gloria stood up and, with that soft Eleanor Roosevelt-like voice, surveyed the disparate throng and said, "Well, we all have one thing in common — a vagina." I jumped about three feet because I had never heard that word outside of my gynecologist's office before.

We were a noisy, busy, pushy group, often suspicious of each other, but thrilled that something was happening. That was the year that the word "networking" was born.

I was fresh from the White House, with good press contacts and some political savvy because if you had covered FDR and Eleanor and worked for LBJ, you couldn't miss. My role was a small one — to handle the press and get us into the newspapers! I had an advantage: It was a slow news period. President Nixon was at the California White House, so we were the hottest news in town. And we had those wonderful seasoned press women who knew a movement when they saw one and who were weary of the handful of women who were news.

I lined up a photo opportunity featuring six or seven new leaders, and sure enough, the next day we were page one — stretching across the *New York Times* and the *Washington Post*.

Meanwhile, out in San Clemente, President Nixon met with his Cabinet. Secretary of State Bill Rogers had flown in that morning, and when he arrived he threw the eastern newspapers onto the table for all to see.

"It looks like vaudeville," someone said.

"Who is Gloria Steinem?" President Nixon asked.

"Oh, she's one of Henry Kissinger's girlfriends," the secretary of state laughed.

Helen Thomas, of UPI, was within hearing distance. She pounced on the words, and the wire stories began to flow. The comment made page one everywhere. In New York, Gloria firmly replied, "I am not now, nor have I ever been one of Henry Kissinger's girlfriends."

The press kept the story moving, and we were here to stay—part of the national political story forever and ever. Thank you, Gloria, for not being Henry Kissinger's girlfriend. Think how history would have been changed. We would all be making cookies.

Everyone has made cookies, but making cookies is all the radical right wants us to do—while the National Rifle Association guns us down. You see, if we are up to our elbows in cookie dough, we can't be at the peace tables, and peacemaking is what we are best at—as Secretary of State Madeleine Albright proves—from family squabbles on up. We will never have peace while the peacemakers are all male. It is disgraceful and ridiculous to think that any peacemaking body can be all male. And making cookies is not the most important thing to do for the children of this country.

Hang in there! Stay gutsy. Make networking a way of life, and make things happen. From those early lessons and actions, we now have seven women in the Senate, 47 in Congress, and two on the Supreme Court. Out in Chicago, Carol Mosely-Braun got the message, ran for the Senate, and was elected.

Things also were happening over at the Supreme

Court, where Associate Justice Ruth Ginsburg asked 17 pertinent questions of the lawyers arguing before that august body. Never before had a brand new justice been so "pushy." Ruth Ginsburg let the Supreme Court know what sexual harassment was all about. It's not all that complicated, she seemed to say, and she laid out the definition: "One sex has to put up with something the other sex doesn't have to put up with. It is different treatment for men and women. Period."

Congresswoman Pat Schroeder, of Colorado, showed up in Congress — 32 years old, briefcase in hand, a husband who was a lawyer, and two small children at her side. When people would ask her husband, "Why aren't YOU the congressman?" he would reply: "We found a better candidate." On the day she walked out on the floor of Congress, looking more like a page than a member, one baffled-looking old codger asked her, "How can you be a congressman and have two small children, too?"

She had her answer ready, and she fired back at him: "Because I have a brain *and* a uterus, and I use both." We learned not to ignore the put-downs, but instead to answer back. And the smart, sensitive men began joining us in our answers. The doors began opening up — not completely — but opening more than they ever had before.

Women in public life were our most visible evidences of equality. We wanted them appointed and we wanted them elected. And we are getting there as mayor, city councilwoman, legislator, and in seven states including this one, a real shot at being governor.

Now is the time, if ever there was a time, when we must stop being pushed around. We cannot fall into their traps. We cannot suck up to them. Life can and should include public action and motherhood.

True, there is a strain in juggling kids and jobs, even in families that don't meet Vice President Quayle's definition of a family. So, in order to pay the bills, I began

writing about my new role, that of an unexpected surrogate mother—two teenagers left to my care by the death
of my brother. *Unplanned Parenthood* was the story of my
golden years. I spoke to my own children, by then grown
and flourishing on the West Coast. Was my having had a
career traumatic for them? Had they hidden psychological
problems from me? Were they still thumb-sucking or bed-
wetting? Both said no, that they had had a great old time
growing up, knowing the strong women who came to our
house. But they thought that maybe it had affected me—
in the head.

We never are going to be all of one mind, but I have
watched very closely as the special interests, the lobbyists,
the sources of campaign funds try to move in and take us
over. You don't have to come out for capital punishment
just because your predecessors have. You don't have to
pose with guns or water down badly needed gun control
legislation to get along with the good old boys. You don't
have to mouth the demands of that frightening growth
industry, contractors for prisons, just to be anti-crime
when you know it is education within the walls that is
needed.

Don't fall for that line "no more taxes," which some
very highly paid PR firms dreamed up for politicians to
tout. You know in your hearts that "no new taxes" means
"no more progress." Cut the fat, yes, but don't cut the
heart.

Hillary Rodham Clinton brought a bipartisan message to Austin last March when she launched her politics-
of-meaning plea. Even Hillary was advised to "just give a
little wave" during the campaign, and she now has proven
that she can become the lion of Capitol Hill hearings.

My friends, it is not fashionable, nor is it good politics, to play things so safe that we kill our chances to make
a difference. There is no reason to be there if you don't
make a difference because the job isn't all that easy or

that much fun. If it is possible to put meaning into politics, it will be done because of the entrance of women in greater, stronger numbers.

Hillary asked us each to redefine ourselves in terms of a new ethos of individual responsibility and caring. Fourteen thousand students and townspeople sat, spellbound, as they listened to that remarkable young woman speak for 45 minutes without notes. She called for a bipartisan effort to get more women into politics, and she turned to some words of the former Republican chairman from a *Life* magazine article that she carries in her wallet. The article was by Lee Atwater, the late chairman of the Republican National Committee, written as he lay dying of cancer. You may have read it, but it bears repeating:

> *"Long before I was struck with cancer, I felt something stirring in American society. It was*

a sense among the people of the country, Repub-
licans and Democrats alike, that something was
missing from their lives, something crucial. I
was trying to position the Republican Party to
take advantage of it, but I wasn't exactly sure
what it was. My illness helped me to see that
what was missing in society is what was miss-
ing in me. A little heart, a lot of brotherhood.

"The '80s were about acquiring—acquiring
wealth, power, prestige. I know. I acquired more
wealth, power and prestige than most, but you
can acquire all you want and still feel empty.
What power wouldn't I trade for a little more
time with my family? What price wouldn't I
pay for an evening with friends? It took a dead-
ly illness to put me eye-to-eye with that truth,
but it is a truth that the country, caught up in
its ruthless ambitions and moral decay, can
learn on my dime.

"I don't know who will lead us through
the '90s, but they must be made to speak to
this spiritual vacuum at the heart of
American society, this tumor of the soul."

That is a lasting legacy from a key player in
American politics. It should alert the rest of us, for we all
could cite examples of what is lacking in our society and,
perhaps, in ourselves. You are the leaders who can make
that happen through a concerted effort to motivate government to operate more thoughtfully and less greedily. The
time is ripe for this movement.

I have seen many stages of the women's movement
since 1971. I have seen it in my own daughter and her
friends of 40 years now who headed for law school,
reached the glass ceilings, and now enjoy the clothes, the
cars, and going to a spa twice a year to keep fit. But when

we talk soul-to-soul, it is that word "meaning" that keeps cropping up. They are burned out, and no endeavor seems to live up to their dreams.

It isn't romance that these bright young baby boomers seek, though that would help. They sense that their long hours and creativity really should count toward significant changes in society. They can't find meaning at the office. They have to find meaning in off-the-job activities — in community work or political activities. The business schools of this country seem to be missing the point by attempting to train future CEOs and inspiring corporations to fill this gap.

Perhaps the lack of meaning on the job comes as a surprise to women because we are fairly new arrivals in the job marketplace. I hope that you take note and use some of your influence and power to help reunite Americans to solve our ills. I hope that you recommend to the business schools of this state that they take a long look at how to counsel the graduates they are turning out on how to achieve meaningful lives.

You women have a lot of time out there to do a whole variety of things. With estimated life expectancies of 79, we have been given the gift of time. I urge you to realize who you are and the power that rests in your hands. Martha Graham, who died at age 96, said it better than anyone: "There is a vitality, a life's force, an energy, a quickening which is translated through you into action. And because there is only one of you in all time, this expression is unique; if you block it, it will never exist and will be lost. The world will never have it."

I urge you to use your energy, your ideals, your profession, your humor, and your commitment to yourself and to the rest of us. In the coming century, it can happen — because of us.

———— ✦✦ ————

My remarks to the Texas Home Economics Association in 1990 provide an interesting look at the evolution of the women's movement throughout the 20th century, the frustration that women felt during the '50s and '60s, and the great strides that we made during the latter part of the century.

━━━━━━━━━━ ━╬╬━ ━━━━━━━━━━

TEXAS HOME ECONOMICS ASSOCIATION
Austin, Texas, February 23, 1990

I am going to talk to you about education, mental health, family, politics, aging, and home economics today. I am going to take you from the last decade into the present one. I am going to talk to you about what women have been and what they are becoming. Maybe hit upon the last century and the next one. And I can't think of any group that embraces the whole ball of wax more than this one. It's downright scary, but a lot of future happiness rides on your shoulders and the creative ways you will find to deal with challenges and guide our institutions in helping families live up to their potentials. Family has been your business since home economics became a discipline.

I want to shout this to the state legislature and to the boards of regents of colleges and universities that make surprise attacks to scatter or kill their home economics departments. We hear a lot about the family, but I ask you, who has been in the middle of it the longest? Since 1860, you've been into family planning, canning, weaving, raising pigs, and milking cows. Now you're into neighborhoods and cities.

Home economists were the first community action program. Who is most experienced to make it happen for them? Who can guide us best to make it all work in a time of two-salaried families and single-parent families, subject to all the well publicized stresses, strains, and traumas that fill the talk shows and nightly news?

Who can make it work for the latchkey kids? For the children in day care? (Incidentally, there are many people in academia who once thought child development was not an appropriate college course. Now colleges are glad that Ph.D.s are given for this course.)

Who can attend to the needs of the growing population of seniors who are living longer and more vitally than ever before? Civilizations are tested by how they treat their young and their old. How does our country measure up? How does Texas measure up? All these groups live better lives because of Texas home economists who have seen families move from traditional problems to untraditional families that require untraditional solutions.

My faith in your profession stems, primarily, from three women whom I have known personally, all marvelous role models: my sister-in-law, my niece Cindy, and Judith Moyers, who is a UT Home Ec grad and the first to brag that being a professional home economist prepared her for each of the four or five careers she has had, including being the wife of Bill Moyers.

I chatted with Judith the other night, and she traced those careers: "I taught 'home ec' in high school. Later, I worked for Texas Electric Service Company in sales promotion. In New York, I was active in the consumer movement, which led to my being selected to serve on several corporate boards as the consumer advocate. Now I am president of Public Affairs TV, which produces Bill's TV shows. I handle insurance, pregnancy leave, and maternity policies for our small company."

She added that she was always a satisfied parent because she felt she was professionally trained for parenthood. Good advice from Judith: Be prepared to hold several careers in life.

It does take elasticity of people and programs to keep up with the world and its fast-moving events. Change must not be resisted. It would be foolish to do that, and change is often needed for progress. The trick is learning to walk hand-in-hand with change and grow with it.

Beginning with the '60s, we underwent great changes within our own country's society—changes that began as grassroots movements and finally moved on to the policy makers: civil rights, the women's movement, youth, and, now, the aging revolution. Never in the history of the world has the family been tested by so many changes as in the past 40 years.

One night last summer, I had the opportunity to think about how much women have grown, about how much more of us are reaching out to touch our society and our power structures. It was an evening made to my liking—gathered together were old friends, journalists, and writers. The hostess had asked several of them to read their own prose. It was Betty Friedan who held us spellbound as she read the opening passages of *The Feminine Mystique*, which set the contemporary women's movement into motion. I hadn't read the passages in 20 years, and Betty said that she had never read them aloud before.

Some of us were old allies from the battle lines for the Equal Rights Amendment. Some were daughters—young women who now are in marketing or law or teaching. I watched their faces, felt the intensity, the pulses quickening as Betty read:

> *"The problem lay buried, unspoken for many years in the minds of American women. It was a strange stirring, a sense of dissatisfaction, a yearning that women suffered in the middle of the 20th Century. Each suburban wife struggled with it alone. As she made the beds, shopped for*

groceries, matched slipcover material, ate peanut butter sandwiches with her children, chauffeured Cub Scouts and Brownies, lay beside her husband at night, she was afraid to ask the silent question: 'Is this all?'

"Millions of words were written about women, for women, in books and articles, all telling them they could desire no greater destiny than to glory in their own femininity. All they must do was devote their lives from earliest girlhood to finding a husband and bearing children. They were taught to pity the neurotic, unfeminine, unhappy women who wanted to be poets or physicists or presidents. Truly feminine women did not want careers, higher education, political rights, the independence and opportunities that

old-fashioned feminists fought for. Some women in their 40s and 50s still remembered painfully giving up those dreams, but most younger women no longer even thought about that.

"By the end of the 1950s, the average marriage age of women in America dropped to 20 and was still dropping. The proportion of women attending college, in comparison with men, dropped from 47 percent in 1920 to 35 percent in 1958. A century earlier, women had fought for higher education; now girls went to college to get a husband. By the mid-50s, 60 percent dropped out of college to marry. Colleges built dormitories for married students, but the students were almost always the husbands. A new degree was instituted for the wives—PHT (Putting Husband Through).

"American girls were getting married in high school. Manufacturers put out brassieres with false bosoms of foam rubber for little girls of ten. An ad for a child's dress, size 3-6x, in the **New York Times** *said: 'She, too, can join the man-trap set.'*

"The U.S. birthrate was overtaking India's. Women who had been advised a third or fourth baby would be born dead or defective were being advised how they might have it anyway. In a 1956 tribute to women, **Life** *magazine rejoiced that women who had once wanted careers were now making careers out of having babies. In a New York hospital, a woman had a nervous breakdown when she found she could not breastfeed her baby. In another hospital, women dying of cancer refused a drug which research proved might save their lives because its side effects were said to be unfeminine.*

*"And across America, women would tell
their doctors, 'I feel as if I don't exist.'
Sometimes she blotted out the problem with
a tranquilizer. Sometimes she thought what
she really needed was to redecorate the house
or move to a better neighborhood or have an
affair or another baby. Sometimes she went
to the doctor with symptoms she could hardly
describe, 'A tired feeling . . . I get so angry with
the children, it scares me . . . I feel like crying
without any reason.'*

*"Doctors called it 'the housewife's syn-
drome' or 'the housewife's blight.' 'I see it so
often lately in these young women with four,
five, and six children who bury themselves in
their dishpans. But it isn't caused by detergent,
and it isn't cured by cortisone.'*

*"The problem that had no name, stirring in
the minds of so many American women, could
no longer be ignored."*

That was the beginning of the story, and we were
all part of the rest, all still part of the story underway.
That dauntless world leader, Golda Meir, once said,
"Those who do not know how to weep with their whole
heart don't know how to laugh either."

Women stopped living on the fringes of life and
moved into midstream.

Home economists of this country may have known
how much more potential women had all along. They had
Ellen Richards as a patron saint, and she warned long
before Betty Friedan: "A worse slavery than the world
knows embitters the lives of thousands of women today,
and they never let it be guessed because they see no way
out, and they take all kinds of petty ways to revenge
themselves."

Our women's movement came to national attention when they decided they had to have political clout to be heard. So, on a July day in 1971, the National Women's Political Caucus was born, and the efforts to bring the rights of women into equality and into the public arena began in all seriousness.

Young women started going to law school and engineering school and medical school. Women of all ages began trying to make their votes count, testifying before committees in Congress and in the state legislatures, shouting sometimes because they *had* to be heard. They started suing for equality when they were mistreated, and they often won. And they started running for office and sometimes were elected. In the '80s, they had learned so much that they really began winning—first in the legislatures, then the city councils and the county governments, and then in the mayors' offices.

We stopped being what Sey Chassler, editor of *Redbook*, called "bonsai women," like the dwarfed ornamental tree. We no longer were placed in a tray to be diminished and acculturated to a society of men. We no longer would be the forgotten women of American history. If the women's revolution of the '60s taught us anything, if the aging revolution of the '80s made us glory in our new life spans to live vitally and longer, it is because we stopped waiting for things to happen to us and began *making* them happen for ourselves and for each other. Networking was a big word. I hope it still is.

We women were reaching for freedom and the right to grow to our full potentials in our own country, in our own families, even as we see it happening now across our TV screens in Eastern Europe, Africa, and ultimately— because freedom may be stalled, but it cannot be stopped— in China.

We marched in the streets, battled in legislatures, won some, lost some, and are still at it—proving that women are fit to be business executives, mayors, members of Congress, and governors. I don't know any leaders of the women's movement who are resting. The strong sense of urgency and commitment, once discovered, is deep within us. I find the old names on pro-choice ads, on civic drives for the environment, mental health, hospitals, and on bigger checks than we ever have written for women candidates for mayor and governor.

Who would have thought in the 1950s that seven major Texas cities would be run by women—good women—all competent and all very much alive? Who would have thought that the Democratic primary for governor of Texas would be led by a housewife of the '50s (hairdo and all) who has proved that running a home is not that different from running an office or a government? And that with good management, you can stay within a budget? And with good common sense, you can provide for our best instincts, not our worst?

I don't pretend to say that life is perfect. Working parents of this country do a juggling act equaled only by a Barnum & Bailey performer and get too little help from government and business. But we are, I believe, living more fully and struggling to fill in the gaps. Human services, so much a part of the Washington I knew, have been put on hold, ironically, by the very people who talk about family values in pious tones, then turn around and short-change day care benefits. Women have received little help in the Reagan and Bush administrations. They seem to think you can turn back the clock to the traditional family of one working dad, one stay-at-home mom, and four well-scrubbed children.

We have left it to the private sector and to scores of school and city services to find the untraditional ways to serve the untraditional family—which is most families.

I have been thinking about mental health, and child guidance centers and care for the aged a lot lately. Texas is under court order to improve education, mental health and prison conditions. A giant step toward finding how to do this was Lieutenant Governor Bill Hobby's anti-crime plan of 1989, which showed clearly how the root problems of crime are intertwined with inadequate education and mental health problems.

The wiser legislators are beginning to pick up on it, and you hear them quoting the figures: Texas spends $3,600 a year to educate a school child and $36,000 a year to keep someone behind bars. Obviously, early detection of behavior disorders and treatment is important to help people realize their full potentials. Obviously, education and job training are essential. We must identify at-risk students early, reduce the dropout rates, and not be stingy with help for mental health. In-prison education programs will help make taxpayers out of tax-eaters.

Yet, we now are being exposed to the shallowest kind of thinking, trick slogans, and candidates "out-macho-ing" each other in the political ads that will be playing in this election year.

You can laugh your head off or wring your hands in despair as you read about the programs that some of the candidates recommend for reducing crime. One recommends a rock pile as a treatment center. (There are no job opportunities for busting rocks.) Another candidate thinks he's the best man for the job because he has killed the most people. He's talking from an empty jail cell, which must be the only one in Texas. There is something wrong with our own mental health if we eat all that garbage without raising our voices. We need some serious discussion about ways to really narrow that gap between the $3,600 a year it costs to educate a kid and the $36,000 it costs to keep someone in jail.

Yes, we are in a new decade, and this is an exciting time to be alive, as we watch the explosion of new freedoms in Eastern Europe and Africa, where they are righting old wrongs. It is time to cheer and applaud, not to be enshrouded in doubt and caution.

We who are 200 years ahead in winning a free society do less than our best if we don't turn to righting our own wrongs. If we are a civilized society, we cannot remain adrift in troubled waters because of some who cloud the issues and some who mouth "No new taxes." Those of you whose professional work lies at the heart of so many of these problems that families face are in key positions to help row us to shore.

———————————— ⊷⊶ ————————————

The contemporary women's movement has caused a good deal of confusion between the sexes as to their rightful roles. In truth, we enter the new millennium with less than ideal relations between men and women.

Men sometimes are hesitant to make commitments because they are intimidated by strong women. Some women are reluctant to put a meal onto the table for fear of turning back the clock and finding themselves stuck in the homemaking arts.

Come on! Neither men nor women need to miss out on a romantic, happy, permanent relationship. If we work together, a lot of loneliness can be avoided. Singles bars, exercise spas, even Sunday bookstores are no substitute for deep, abiding friendship and lifelong companionship.

Clare Boothe Luce once warned: "When someone treats you as his inferior, you can be sure that he no longer loves you, if indeed he ever did."

What can bring us together? A little give-and-take, a little humor, and a lot of love. With effort and understanding by us all—men and women—we can achieve great things in our individual lives and for our country.

I do not believe, however ominous this year looks, that the United States will turn back the clock for women on choice. The new Supreme Court can reverse it, they can delay it, they can try to gag the clinics by denying Title X money, they can veto legislation that would prevent this. But somehow, ultimately, choice will prevail because it is the right thing to do. —L.C.

13

SPEECHES FOR WORTHY CAUSES

Carol Channing once sang, "I stand for motherland, America, and a hot lunch for orphans." Speakers find themselves cheering for so many causes. Among my favorites are Planned Parenthood, mental health, and the arts.

———— ✦✦ ————

PLANNED PARENTHOOD LUNCHEON
Houston, Texas, January 22, 1992

Through the years, I have been invited to speak to every kind of group you can imagine, and I often wonder why I was chosen. But today, I know why you wanted to hear from me.

You found out that I am into Planned Parenthood. Yes, at 71 years of age, I have become a born-again mother. Last fall, I inherited two teenagers to raise. My late brother, Tom Sutherland, raised ten children in two batches. By now, seven are grandmothers, and the rest are just out of Play-Doh. And I won the Publisher's Clearinghouse Sweepstakes. (Actually, I *need* to win the sweepstakes and am counting on it tonight.)

Anyway, I was chosen by fate and luck and default to raise these two kids. It has been eye-opening. Every kid deserves to be loved and to be educated, and that is why planning to make room for them is essential.

Amazing how long it has taken the world to come to terms with one of the great destroyers—population. It will surprise you, as it did me, that Lyndon Johnson, the 36th president of the United States, was the very first president to use the words "population control" in a State of the Union address.

So, my dear friends of Houston, that's where I am coming from. You now know about me, and I want you to know that I long have known about you.

I first learned how chic and avante garde the Houston chapter of Planned Parenthood was years ago when "The Best Little Whorehouse in Texas" opened here. Someone had the idea for you to hold the opening night premiere and benefit, and it was a whopping success. It gave respectable citizens like George and Alice Brown and Jake and Terry Hershey—and people even more upright than them—an excuse to attend something that they were dying to see, but wouldn't dare, otherwise.

Now, lesser Planned Parenthood chapters would have been too squeamish to take on the premiere of this particular show as a vehicle for raising funds because of its title. But *NOT* Houston—the wonderful and lusty, spunky and savvy, City of the Southwest. Only in Houston would Planned Parenthood use "The Best Little Whorehouse in Texas" as a fundraising event.

I also know that you were the original home chapter of Barbara and George Bush, who have denied you ever since, but WE remember back when he was on the floor of the Congress saying, "We need to make 'population' and 'family planning' household words. We need to take the sensationalism out of this topic, so it no longer can be used by militants who have no real knowledge of the voluntary nature of the programs, but rather are using it as a political stepping stone."

Right on, George. Come home to the old chapter, and all is forgiven.

I was terrified to read in Maxine or Betsy's columns (and haven't both of them been good friends to this organization?) that I was expected to make a funny speech here today.

Well, I phoned every funny friend I have and asked, "How do you be funny at a planned parenthood meeting?"

Billy Porterfield thought of a new tack: Push planned marriages.

Molly Ivins said, "Liz, whatever you do, skip the coat hanger gags."

But I ask you, can't we restore humor at this point in the history of American politics? In this crisis of choice? We have to!

Take a look at the last two centuries of American political history. We have come from Tom Paine to Thomas Jefferson to David Duke and Randall Terry. So much for Darwin's theory of evolution!

We rub our eyes and wonder: Has the religious right stolen the Republican Party? Has the gag rule silenced the Democrats in Congress?

We who believe in freedom have had to learn to laugh during this tedious waiting period—waiting for

the new Supreme Court to show itself on the issue.
Waiting to see if President Bush will veto yet another
bill to ensure the freedom women thought they had won.

How do we keep our own spirit during this waiting
period? Laughter is a valuable tool. Let me suggest that
you employ both humor and some well-worded ridicule.

The Operation Rescue groups are laughable because
they are so ridiculous, tragic because they are so merciless.

I do not believe, however ominous this year looks,
that the United States will turn back the clock for women
on choice. The new Supreme Court can reverse it, they can
delay it, they can try to gag the clinics by denying Title X
money, they can veto legislation that would prevent this.
But somehow, ultimately, choice will prevail because it is
the right thing to do.

All my life, I've been a working citizen. My faith
does not allow me to believe that any Greater Power has
willed us to be so ignorant that we are willing to crowd
this planet with a lot of suffering babies and children. I
salute you all for having a conscience and a commitment
about that!

MENTAL HEALTH ASSOCIATION OF AUSTIN
Austin, Texas, February 14, 1990

Friends, award winners —

Happy Valentine's Day! Congratulations, and thank
you for all you are doing and for all that you will do.

Since Elizabeth Young invited me to come today, I
have been "getting educated" by reading the association's
material. What particularly caught my eye is a new pro-
gram-in-the-making called "Phone Friend." It is well
written, and I hope it gets going soon.

Visualize yourself in this situation: You are nine
years old, at home alone after school. There's a bad rain-

storm, with thunder and lightning. The roof starts leaking on the kitchen stove. What do you do? Mom is in a meeting at work and can't be disturbed. Dad is out of town on business. There is no one else to call. What do you do?

Probably nothing. Being alone and afraid when you are nine makes it hard to think, but if you had someone to call, someone who would listen and suggest how to handle the situation, you would feel much better, and you'd be proud that you had solved a problem.

Or maybe you've come home to a house that you wish were not empty, but you also dread Dad and Mom coming home. They yell at each other a lot and talk about divorce. You think that maybe it's your fault, and your stomach starts to hurt. If only there was someone to call, someone to talk to, someone to listen.

The "Phone Friend" program started at a women's college in Pennsylvania and has been very successful wherever it has been established. It faces right up to the facts of our modern life: that families today are not traditional, with a working papa, a stay-at-home mama, and two well-scrubbed children. Untraditional methods are necessary to deal with untraditional problems.

Practicing creative friendship can make a big difference in our society. People with tiny voices—children, the aged—have the hardest times being heard. I sincerely hope that the "Phone Friend" program will be under way soon and that its phone number will be publicized widely in the schools and the parents' workplaces. That would be reaching out and touching someone in a way that really would count in this community.

Helping each other by forming creative, alert friendships is a challenge that is gaining a whole set of untraditional volunteers—our older citizens. All of us have been given the gift of time. Our life expectancies have given us an additional 20 years, if we are lucky and stay off Allegheny Airlines. At the time I was born in 1920, I was expected to live to be 63, following the pattern of the women in my family, who all died at age 63 or 65.

Thanks to medical science, we now expect to live to be 75 to 80 years of age. Indeed, a study is underway of Americans who are still working and earning their own livings after age 65. I am proud to be one of the guinea pigs. I'm even prouder that, at age 69, I am one of the younger ones.

The study has turned up a large number of people age 90 and over who are still working, among them a 100-year-old—a chemist in New York who works in his lab three days a week—and I fervently hope that he has a young assistant who checks the formulas. There is the playwright George Abbott, now 102 years old, who is still going to work (hopefully, driven by someone else) and producing.

The "aging revolution" has produced a whole new pool of experienced citizens who have knowledge of people in need. Why are older people particularly valuable? Because they have been tested in the trial fields of life—because sometimes in our lives, we have been weak and been wrong, and we have learned empathy and understanding, and we have a talent for putting problems into perspective. Taking time to listen to another person's anxieties is a big contribution to humanity.

"It is odd," Lady Bird Johnson once said in a memorable quote, "that you get so anesthetized by your own problems that you don't quite fully share the hell of someone close to you."

Being a practicing, creative friend is a subject that is very much on the minds of older people today. They find the old sayings to be true: "Who brings his neighbor's barque to land will find his own has reached the shore"; "The giver is the receiver."

I don't have to tell you that Texas—Austin—is awash with troubled people today. We know people who are in personal financial trouble and just may not make it. Never in my wildest dreams did I think that I would have a friend suffering from AIDS or a friend confined in a penitentiary, but I do—close friends, in both instances. Those things came to be along with the ills of the past decade, with bank failures and Texas' own economic trauma.

Telephone calls, greeting cards (there's a challenge—Hallmark hasn't come up with the card for someone in jail yet), letters written on a regular basis—all of these are lifelines that any one of us can give to those in need. Using your creativity for the benefit of others is a wonderful alternative to dwelling on your own problems. The process is life-enhancing.

Everyone has suffered from depression at one time or another—loss, loneliness, conflicts with people that we love are common causes—and we are blessed if we have friends to take the initiative to get us help.

In my own life, it was a year to the day after my husband died that I broke out in a terrible case of shingles, which was symptomatic that grief was enshrouding me. I had an alert daughter who made an appointment and drove me to the office of the lady psychiatrist who saw me at the end of the day. For six sessions, I talked through my life, my feelings—pretty dramatic stuff, I thought. Actually, spellbinding. What really was insulting was that the psychiatrist often would lapse off into sleep as I talked. (I can't stand audiences like that.) Every time she awoke, though, she gave me a line or a thought to hang on to. Maybe she wasn't sleeping, but praying for me. Anyway, at the sixth session, I ran out of things to say, and I told her so.

"Fine," she said, "I think your ego is intact now, and here is my home number in case you need me." I never did, though, because her training and wisdom had led me, without my realizing it, to talk through my problems and discover the answers myself.

So, I picked up my intact ego and came home to Texas, where I have lived happily ever after.

Humor is essential to a sense of well-being. Laughter recharges us thoroughly. It activates every cell, and we come alive. It restores us, both physically and emotionally.

At the University of Texas, I was a young, green cub reporter on *The Daily Texan*. One day I was assigned to get right over to the UT Board of Regents' meeting because something "BIG" was about to happen, and it did. In an awesome room in the Main Building sat a fragile, shy lady in a black dress with a high, white lace collar. She held a small notebook in her hand with her brief statement written out by her own hand, words that set in motion a whole revolution toward mental health treatment in this state.

"The common goals of my late brother, Will, and I are to use our funds in the field of mental hygiene." Thus, the Hogg Foundation was born that day in 1940 and since then has guided modern approaches to mental health care across the state. The lady, of course, was Miss Ima Hogg.

How was she drawn to this cause, over so many other needs? As a teenager in the 1900s, she suffered from "insomnia, anxieties and mild depression" and sought treatment in the East at the Institution of Learning. There, she learned about modern approaches to mental health and saw the good that could be done by psychologists, psychiatrists, social workers, and enlightened citizens. In 1929 the Child Guidance Center was established in Houston, thanks to Miss Ima and a group of dedicated women. Today it is one of the biggest and best children's centers for mental health care in the country.

Miss Ima was the first in Texas to set a benchmark for progressive mental health care, a tradition that you, as an organization, have continued. Your group is doing valuable work instituting and refining various programs that help people live up to their full potentials. Go for it.

"WHITE HOUSE FOLKLORE AS I HAVE KNOWN IT"
The Art Center of Waco
Waco, Texas, April 14, 2000

Friends, I often have thought that if the White House were advertised for rent, the ad might read: "Available for four-year lease, large furnished white house in downtown Washington on 18 acres of landscaped lawns. Within a stone's throw of everything and everyone. Offers sweeping view of the Potomac River. Contains 132 rooms, 21 baths and 69 closets, 1 (sometimes more) doghouses, tennis court, bowling alley, theater, swimming pool, and treehouse. Priceless antiques and paintings. Available for only four years at a time, as landlord is known to be fickle."

I have done time in that great White House as a reporter covering eleven presidents in all and as a staff member for five years during the Johnson Administration. I don't know whether that says how old I am or how young our country is.

Even now, more than a half century since I first arrived in Washington at the age of 22, I remain fascinated, swept up in its pulsating history — 200 years of drama — from the chilly November when Abigail Adams moved in to now, as Hillary Clinton moves out to run for the United States Senate. (Both Abigail and Hillary were lame ducks. Both of them could have used an Equal Rights Amendment, and both of them supported one.)

In the years that followed, Washington has been called many things, such as "the only asylum in the world run by its own inmates" and "the dazzling City on the Hill." The description of that majestic city that I like best, though, is the one given by a fellow reporter, Allen Drury, in his novel *Advise and Consent*: "Washington — that great white marbled capital where good men do evil and evil men do good in a way that only Americans can understand—and often they are baffled."

In her diary, Lady Bird Johnson described her arrival at the White House: "History thunders down the corridors at you," she said, prophetically, the day we drove down from the Johnsons' home, "The Elms." It was 15 days after President Kennedy's assassination, and Lady Bird entered the White House as its new occupant, along with her husband, the 36th president of the United States. "At first, you walk around on tiptoes and talk in whispers. Finally, you relax and take up your duties. Entering and leaving, you are aware constantly that each room, each object, holds history in its hand."

The White House has been a place for collecting everything—furniture, paintings, animals, stamps, wedding gifts, contributions for Iran-Contra. It has known moments of national tragedy, of national scandal, of heady achievement, and of deep disappointment.

At the time I arrived in Washington one June day in 1942, in the midst of a nation at war, the White House was the home of the family of Franklin Roosevelt. I qualified for a White House press pass that allowed me to cover the president, and I was admitted to Mrs. Roosevelt's press conferences, held every few weeks on the second floor. There, we received our news, a cup of tea, and a social conscience from the regal, compassionate Eleanor Roosevelt.

I never had seen such a large tea service—certainly not in Salado, Texas, where I was born—nor had I ever met such smart women as activist Frances Perkins, the first woman ever in a presidential Cabinet, and Ellen Woodward, head of the Social Security Administration.

Eleanor was the first first lady to be available to the press as an obligation. She allowed only women to attend these meetings and, by discriminating, she wiped out discrimination. AP, the *New York Herald Tribune*, and any other media organization that wanted to keep up with Eleanor as a newsmaker had to hire a woman, and once we had a toehold in the door, we hung on to it.

Of course, today that wouldn't be done. By the time Lady Bird was a first lady, those who wrote about her numbered about 85, both men and women.

I was the first professional newswoman to hold the job of press secretary to a first lady, and that included all stories emerging from the East Wing—briefly, women, dogs, and old brocades. In my time, there were two White House weddings, and they were big stories.

Americans are intensely interested in everything about the White House—its furnishings, the entertainment at receptions and dinners, the children who live there, and the animals that the first family brings with them. The public wants to know about everything, from Calvin Coolidge's one-eyed chicken to Chelsea Clinton's cat, which appeared on a campaign button even before the Clintons arrived at the White House.

Speaking of Calvin Coolidge, a friend once asked him kiddingly, as they strolled past the White House, "Who lives there?" Coolidge replied, *"No one."* In fact,

everyone does. Almost every American has a sense of personal possession about that house.

Time and the 41 families who have resided in the White House fill the place with memories and ghosts of those who have gone before.

George Washington never slept there. He watched it go up, but was out of office before it was finished. I suspect that no one has slept in the White House except Coolidge, who required eleven hours a night and got them.

Most of the men who have lived there spend fitful nights fretting, tossing, turning, telephoning about the nation's problems, wondering what their predecessors would have done about current problems.

"Now, it is 4:00 A.M., and ghosts walk," wrote Allen Drury. "See them pass across the counterpane of the man who likes awake there. See them pass, calm, frozen into history, all passion spent, all battles over, defeats, and victories.

"He may ask, 'Would you have bought Louisiana?' 'Would you have put upon the South the moral burden of opening conflict?' 'Would you have taken Panama— or given it back?' 'Would you have maneuvered Japan into striking first?'"

Updating that, "Would you have risked the hydrogen bomb to shorten the war?" "Would you have sent the troops into Korea, Tonkin Bay, or Kosovo?" "Should you have answered the unrelenting press as it envelops you with personal questions?" "Should you send back the six-year-old who was rescued and brought to our shores to the dubious fate of Cuba and Castro?"

Little wonder that in the turbulent '60s, LBJ turned to some of his advisers and pointed out: "If there were easy solutions, they wouldn't get to the president. That's what presidents are for—he gets the tough ones."

The White House also is a museum displaying an ongoing collection of fine paintings and furnishings.

During the Kennedy years, 307 examples of American furniture had been acquired, as well as 266 objects of glassware, ceramics, and metalware. All of these additions reflected the history of the decorative arts of our country. Seventy-four oil paintings and watercolors were added to the collection.

The collection continued into the Johnson years, widening in scope and always rich in quality. The first donation—a Sheffield silver coffee urn that had been bought by John Adams and acquired by a Boston silver fancier—was given to us because of, well, the Pakistani camel driver that LBJ had picked up in a vice-presidential visit to Karachi. In Texas style, LBJ invited him to Texas, giving me the job of raising the money to bring him and escorting him from Washington to the LBJ Ranch and on to Kansas City to meet President Truman.

He came, with the help of the "People to People" program. The Boston silver collector who headed the program, Mark Bortman, felt that the camel driver's visit had won such friends throughout Asia that he decided to part with his valuable silver coffee urn, in order to honor LBJ. Of course, we held a ceremony to receive, once again, for the White House the very coffee urn that its first occupants, John and Abigail Adams, had used there.

Of course, the White House collections didn't begin with the Kennedys or the Johnsons, but with John and Abigail Adams. It has been 200 years since Abigail—already three years into her role as first lady—arrived at the White House by coach on a cold November day in 1800. She had a hard time finding the place and became lost several times in the woods of Maryland along the way.

Thank goodness for the Adamses' letter-writing habits. We rely heavily on Abigail's letters written to Quincy, Massachusetts, back home, for early descriptions of the White House. The plaster walls were still wet when she arrived. There was no wood and no one to cut it. It would take 40 cords of wood to dry the place out. There were no bells to summon the 30 servants, and she had to use the great ballroom—now called the East Room—as a place to hang her wash. She gave us ringing descriptions, though: "This house was built for the ages."

And so it has been.

In government books, the White House is listed as "Park Service Reservation No. 1." The building and grounds are tended and maintained by the United States Department of the Interior and the National Park Service. There is a Fine Arts Commission and a White House Historical Association. And since John Adams's time, steps have been taken—however faltering—to keep it intact through the efforts of a host of other committees and commissions.

The White House is the office and residence of the chief executive, the setting for receiving foreign visitors who come to call, and it is the home of a family. The glare of the world's spotlight never dims in the White House. The phones never stop ringing. Dignitaries from the world's 167 nations are continually ushered in and out for State visits. And in between all this bustle, the milestones of the lives of first families are observed—graduations, weddings, births, funerals.

Presidents have taken steps to preserve the White House's history and possessions ever since John Adams ordered the first inventory. Keeping it intact sometimes presented problems.

In the beginning, John and Abigail had to bring much of their own furniture and linens to the White House by oxcart. Indeed, if you go to Boston today, I urge you to go out to nearby Quincy and visit the Adams family home of both John and John Quincy, which contains some of the personal belongings that resided for a time in the White House. It is one of the best-preserved presidential homes, certainly the most historic, since it housed two presidents. The vast library that this brilliant, creative family owned is there and might be considered the first presidential library.

There were other historic milestones concerning the possessions of the White House. In 1812, when the Madisons lived there, the British set fire to the place. Before fleeing, Dolly oversaw the saving of the most valuable possessions — the two giant Gilbert Stuart portraits of Martha and George Washington. The British troops ransacked the house from cellar to garret, drank the wine, and put a torch to the furniture, provisions, groceries, and an excellent library that had cost President Madison $12,000 to assemble.

The Madisons never moved back into the house. When Madison's successor, James Monroe, moved in, he found that the partially rebuilt house contained few comforts and no elegance. Monroe, who had served the country in Europe, added clocks, a set of silver-plated flatware, and the handsome vermeil centerpiece tableau of epergnes, candlesticks, and bowls that is still used today.

Ghosts of old do continue to haunt the possessions. One morning, when Lady Bird went to the government warehouse with J. B. West, the chief usher, she came upon a trunk with "James Monroe" written on the front. When she opened it, she saw that it was very carefully built to pack and carry the pieces of that famous vermeil that Monroe had purchased in Paris.

She told me that there also was a wheelchair, perhaps the one that President Wilson used during his long, last weary months in the White House.

Fire is not the only way things disappeared at the White House.

President Chester A. Arthur didn't like the furnishings and appointments. He swept up 24 wagonloads, and all of it — carpets, curtains, chandeliers, pots, and pans — went under the hammer. Indeed, the auction was so complete that one newspaper reported "the sale of a rat trap that caught the rat, that ate the suit, that belonged to Mr. Lincoln."

Historically, the furniture was important, but in fact, the reason for the big sale was that President Arthur was a dandy and wanted more stylish things. With Louis Comfort Tiffany's help, he selected the Ottoman and Turkish period furniture—tassels on everything! Tiffany designed a massive screen that stretched from the State Dining Room to the East Room, making the house very dark. You can be sure that when Teddy Roosevelt came in, he got rid of that!

During the Johnson years, a wealth of paintings were added to the White House's walls by donors, many of whom were personal friends of LBJ and Lady Bird. One favorite was a watercolor, "Surf at Prout's Neck," by Winslow Homer. The painting was done in 1893 and showed off this famous artist's talents for the first time. The works of such American artists as Thomas Sully, Mary Cassatt, Thomas Eakins, and Thomas Moran also were added, as well as many portraits of former presidents and first ladies.

When first we arrived there in 1963, Lady Bird was advised to have the president's portrait done early in his term. The signs of strain and stroke that are so clear in the portrait of Woodrow Wilson were lesson enough.

Lady Bird worked hard at getting this busy, never-sit-still man to pose. Madame Shoumatoff, who had done the last portrait of FDR, dramatically posed in his Navy cloak, was commissioned for the painting. She was a remarkably interesting woman who had been an artist for 60 years, and she kept the president fascinated as she told him interesting stories about her escape from Russia during the Revolution. LBJ was pleased with the portrait, and Madame Shoumatoff was delighted.

The next afternoon, the curator, Jim Ketchum,

received a frantic call from her asking if he could come up to the second floor where the portrait had been completed. He took the elevator to the second floor, rapped gently on the door, and, upon entering, discovered a rather strange scene.

There, on an easel, was the finished portrait of LBJ, and throughout the room on hangers and garment racks were various outfits from the president's wardrobe. Madame Shoumatoff was frantic. It seems that the president was so pleased with her first portrait that he wanted five more, each in different apparel. He had selected the outfits himself and asked the valet to lay them out so Madame could begin. She stood there wringing her hands in anticipation of painting him five more times. Jim Ketchum remembers her words vividly: "A Xerox machine, Mr. Ketchum. Zee president sinks I am a Xerox machine."

China is another favorite element of the White House collection. The emerald-rimmed Truman china was becoming depleted, and White House dinners were growing to 160 and sometimes 220 guests, so Lady Bird began making plans for a larger set of White House china. She wanted to use the wildflowers of the United States for the pattern, and she worked with Tiffany and Company to undertake the project. They did a brilliant job—except for the dessert plates, on which the wildflowers were off-center.

Tiffany agreed to replace them and, of course, we knew that meant that these 250 dessert plates had to be destroyed, so no one would exploit them in the open market. It was the curator, Jim Ketchum, and the social secretary, Bess Abell, who came up with a plan. They found a cement basement room, placed sketches of a very unpopular aide on the wall, and gathered the staff to pitch plates. In less than an hour, the mission was accomplished.

A word about presidents and first ladies who were collectors themselves:

Teddy Roosevelt, the big-game hunter, filled the house with stuffed game. He placed moose heads in the State Dining Room. When Woodrow Wilson arrived, he hated looking up at moose heads while he was dining, so he rearranged the room to put the moose heads at his back.

Florence Harding collected little elephants and had them following each other around the family's private quarters — on coffee tables, chairs, bookshelves, and floors. Edith Wilson collected old, large feather fans. Julia Tyler collected her trademark, the headbands. She always wore a headband with a jewel right in the middle. While in mourning, she replaced the diamond with ebony. Dolly Madison had a snuffbox collection, and she used her own snuffbox as an icebreaker, offering it to guests. Mrs. Hoover collected expensive Chinese vases, now on display in the Hoover Library. FDR had a famous stamp collection.

John F. Kennedy collected autographs and scrimshaw teeth. Once, when Jackie invited Greta Garbo to dinner, the president showed her his scrimshaw collection. After that, anytime anyone asked Garbo what she remembered most about the White House exhibit, she would reply, "the president's teeth."

Lady Bird brought her own collection of Lowestoft china and Boehm birds to the Yellow Room during her stay. Betty Ford didn't collect anything, but she had a delightful way of making sure the servants were cleaning thoroughly. She would put cigarette butts between the fingers of statues to see how long it would take for them to be removed.

PART II

Now for the
Nitty-Gritty

Those who write speeches for the big shots of the high-tech world must speak to the world. So young and so immersed in racing for the "new, new thing," some of these folks think that anything that predates the 386 microprocessor is ancient history. I suspect a few of them even think Gerald Ford is an automobile executive.

—L. C.

14

TIPS FOR SPEAKING TO HIGH-TECH GROUPS

Our early presidents and public figures were afraid to use humor, for fear someone would laugh at our new fledgling country. Today, corporate types—who need to be taken seriously by the public and their stockholders—have the same fear. It is hard to laugh about an oil spill or a Tylenol bottle, and there are very few worthwhile jokes about tobacco or computers.

As we enter the new millennium, the need for vision from the private sector that goes beyond the stockholders is greater than ever. The Internet puts us all within reach of one another. We all are pedaling fast to keep up with today's explorers: the high-tech crowd.

Don't underestimate your role in the whole span of things. Actually, speechwriters help to shape policy, and you can't serve your client well if you're isolated in a small cubbyhole across town. Speechwriters actually can help to steer the ship—whether the vessel is a company, a branch of government, or an organization—if you are in on mapping out the journey.

Those who write speeches for the big shots of the high-tech world must speak to the world. So young and so immersed in racing for the "new, new thing," some of these folks think that anything that predates the 386 microprocessor is ancient history. I suspect a few of them even think Gerald Ford is an automobile executive.

Speechwriters for high-tech executives, many of whom live and work in the Silicon Valley's new frontier—my hometown of Austin—are striving harder to get their clients to view the world through a wider lens, at least in their speeches. They tell me that they have to grab moments with these young executives in order to glean material that will humanize their speeches—sometimes in a car, an elevator, over a quick coffee.

Most people like to talk about themselves when they feel comfortable doing so. In her book, Barbara Walters tells a story about a dinner party where she was seated next to Aristotle Onassis, who was known to be a difficult conversationalist. Barbara asked him how he made his first dollar. He was good through dessert.

Unaccustomed as they are to speaking outside their own high-tech vocabulary, the wisest leaders in the computer crowd are beginning to offset their distant, billionaire images by highlighting their sizable charitable gifts. In doing so, they humanize themselves and make themselves part of their communities.

Michael Dell, Austin's youthful head of Dell Computer Corporation, and his wife, Susan, led the way for major gifts from their own top "Dellionaires" to museums for children and the arts, as well as for a major new center for aging citizens. One of these forward-thinking philanthropists explained, "Dell wants its success to add to the quality of life in Austin."

Bill Gates is using some of his billions to fund scholarships for minorities, children's immunization programs, and computer equipment for disadvantaged students.

All of these gifts say, "I care." Those of you who write speeches for corporate types should take full advantage of these types of activities and use them in your speeches. They're excellent examples of the meat that goes in the middle of the speech (remember #2).

High-tech speeches present a perfect opportunity to inspire the audience, a great venue for "waving the flag at the end," as my formula goes.

Who wouldn't like to hear about the long-term vision of a business executive facing a fresh millennium, with the aid of the Internet and global networking? Experts such as Robert Rubin say that globalization has remarkably changed how we live, making the world's populace far more interdependent today than one hundred years ago. Yet, these advances also widen the gulf between the haves and the have-nots, and each set becomes increasingly aware of their own identity.

Cyberspace is wide open for explanation—totally unexplored by the average speaker or listener.

What will cyberspace be like? I want to hear it from the experts. Lacking that, I tapped into my best cyberspace sources, who are either students or beginners in the computer trade, and here are their predictions:

1. You'll never see money again. I can adjust to that; it's not so different from growing up during the Great Depression.

2. Of course, when you finally take the plunge and decide to purchase something online, you type in your credit card number, take a deep breath, click the mouse, and pray that a hacker doesn't see your numbers in the transaction.

You don't know until you get your statement and can't remember buying ten garden tools in Vermont.

3. Will this make us less trusting and free in what we say? I fear it will. Anything you e-mail at work is subject to exposure. You can be subpoenaed, based on your flippant comments to a co-worker.

The high-tech industry needs to show that it has vision and integrity, not just economic muscle. That is the role of the intrepid young executives who lead this vast new fast-track world. Their challenge is to break through the Great Digital Divide and help us to understand its potentials on a human scale. It is possible that the chips can lead us to health, instead of hunger; population control, instead of population explosion; and, yes, even to ultimate peace, instead of war.

(Can you spot that flag waving?)

High-tech executives have the power to make the world a little better by giving fairness, compassion, and concern for the common good the same weight as earnings per share, P/E ratios, and the Consumer Price Index.

"Civilization," as Bill Moyers told a University of Texas graduating class, "is a web of cooperation joining people to family, friends, communities, and country, creating in the individual, a sense of reliance on the whole . . . through powerful loyalties to the common good."

The United States has on tap brilliant leaders in both public and private voices. We have the freedom and access to an international dialogue.

This is a great hour for the human race. We all are needed. A century ago, Emerson wrote, "We think our civilization is near its meridian, but we are yet only at the cockcrowing and morning star."

Let us reach for the stars!

For most of us, life is an epic novel in progress, divided into a series of sagas—our own mini-series in the making, rife with disappointments and heady successes, a story of adventures, daring defeat, and dogged determination amid troubles and turmoil. So it has been with my own life.

—L. C.

15

RECYCLING YOUR WORDS AND ANECDOTES: HOW TO USE THE "SAGAS OF LIFE"

If you give speeches often, as I do, one of the most helpful hints I can give you is to *recycle your words and anecdotes*.

Not every speech has to be an original. If certain remarks and stories that you've used in the past played well, then by all means, use them again. Once you have developed a basic speech that contains winning comments and stories, it's easy to adapt it to fit specific audiences or situations by lengthening it or shortening it, tweaking it with quotes or specific life experiences that link you to the group you are addressing.

Over the years, I've found that people usually are more interested in hearing about my life than about an assigned subject. So, I've developed a basic speech that I call my "Sagas of Life."

I believe that life is lived in sagas, or segments, dramatically defined by the series of events within each time period. My own life has developed roughly in three 25-year sagas that became the outlines for my three previous books: *Ruffles and Flourishes*, the story of my years in Washington and the White House; *Getting Better All the Time*, which told about my life during the post-LBJ years when aging and widowhood came; and then *Unplanned Parenthood: The Confessions of a Seventysomething Surrogate Mother*, the tale of my experiences raising my brother's teenagers after his death.

The speech that follows is one that I have used many times by adapting it to fit a specific occasion or group. I refer to it as my "Sagas of Life" speech or my "accordion" speech because I can easily abbreviate my remarks, if time is running short, or lengthen it, if I need to fill in before the next segment of the program.

THE "SAGAS OF LIFE"
("Accordion" Speech)

Friends, you want me to talk about life, as I have known it? What I have learned through living and writing is that every lifetime, every family, offers a series of sagas — an epic novel in progress, a mini-series in the making, a story of adventure, daring and defeat, sometimes dogged determination, sometimes heady success. Often, life is a search for peace of mind in the midst of troubles and turmoil.

Life has been good to me, taken me to exciting places and into actions of which I had never dreamed. So, being a storyteller and reporter by training, I have written about it. Had I been an artist, I would have put it onto canvas. Had I been a songwriter, I might have written a ballad. But I am a storyteller by heritage and training.

The sagas of my life are represented in my three books, each covering about 25 years.

My first book, *Ruffles and Flourishes*, took me from birth in Salado, Texas, through my education at the University of Texas at Austin, to the White House of Eleanor and Franklin Roosevelt when I was 22, and through the following years, the Kennedy assassination and the White House of Lyndon and Lady Bird Johnson. It is the warm and tender story of a simple girl from Texas who found adventure in the White House. It ends in January of 1969, just as Richard Nixon's limousine rounded the corner of 15th and Pennsylvania Avenue, and we departed Washington, D.C.

Doubleday signed me to write the story of how a young reporter had turned into a White House press secretary. The book was perfect for reliving those busy years of White House days, and it was a good thing that I was busy writing, since all those lovely invitations from embassies and other fancy places had suddenly stopped.

I wrote about the weddings, whistlestop trains (my favorite time), travels, and river raft rides down the Snake River or the Rio Grande with flotillas of reporters in the wake, about the state dinners and historic moments, such as the time when Christina Ford and Secretary of Defense Bob McNamara were into such a spirited twist in the East Room that she popped a bosom out of the top of her strapless dress! Those are times that live on when the flower arrangements and menus are forgotten.

The second saga and book, *Getting Better All the Time*, came when I left Washington in 1976, after my husband's death, to return to my Texas roots, after 34 heady years of that remarkably exciting city. *Getting Better* is about aging, facing widowhood, and changing an attitude of despair and loneliness into a chance at a second life. In writing that book, I found a large audience of widows who yearned for positive thinking and a network of friends.

Statistics tell us that women will spend one-third of their lives alone due to divorce, death, or a variety of other reasons. Loneliness and isolation are the hazards. It was another widow who gave me some sensible advice that I have passed on to many others: "Think of it this way—God has given you a chance at another life."

Returning to Texas—to Austin—and fixing up my own launching pad for this new life was life-enhancing. It freed me to put aside the past, to enjoy the present, and to look to the future. In today's world, a network of friends is essential. Families are scattered. Renewing old friendships and initiating new ones was easy. Literature, sports, and even a "Bay at the Moon" group such as mine—however ridiculous—are the answers.

Thirteen years ago, at a ranch near Austin, I sat around a campfire by the river with a group of my cohorts listening to the coyotes yipping and howling. Soon we saw beady eyes at the edge of the firelight. The sights and sounds charmed us and inspired us to start the "Bay at the Moon Club," a regular meeting where we would bring a covered dish and a piece of literature to discuss.

One of the great joys of old age is shocking your children—and baying at the moon does it.

From age 65 on, I was in the happy hour of my life—entertaining, traveling, writing—when circumstances handed me an unplanned situation that became an unplanned book.

It happened when I was 71 and virtually on my way to the nursing home, the cemetery, and, hopefully, heaven. God knows I deserve heaven. My oldest brother died. He was 79—a rogue, a charmer who took the Bible's call to "go forth and multiply" literally. I don't know who said that—Isaiah, Moses—but it was lousy advice for any prophet who recommended a way to solve problems in an overcrowded world. Ten kids in all, he had, and two ex-wives. The first batch of children was grown—mothers and grandmothers themselves. I inherited the second batch, who came to live with me—young teenagers, three of them: Mary, 11; Tommy, 14; and Liz, 16.

Teenagers! The least understood age of all, from 13 to 19, when minds ebb and flow, muscles stretch, feet tap nervously, hormones rage—and testing, testing, testing begins, as all the demands of the world invade your neighborhood and schools. No age is so perplexing—or so ignored.

No one else stepped up to the plate, so there I was, into recycled motherhood again. I happened to be at the Southwest Conference on Aging, where a longtime friend, Erma Bombeck, was receiving an award. (Incidentally, she said it was a case of mistaken identity and, if Willard

Scott called up and wished her *happy birthday*, she would report it as an obscene phone call.)

I told her what was happening—that I was a born-again mom. She replied quickly, "If it's adventure you want, Liz, why not climb Mount Rushmore, tie a rope on Lincoln's wart and do a bungee jump?"

In the weeks that followed, I discovered that the '90s held perils that I don't remember from raising my own teenagers in the '60s.

I found myself spending more time in the grocery store than the manager. I couldn't fill them up. I found that the shortest time span in existence is between loading the kids into the car pool for school and the onset of their rock bands on the car radio. It makes you grateful for a hearing impairment!

And, as time passed, I also discovered:

- Many 13-year-olds only enter and exit a house through windows.

- Many 15-year-olds can go a year without speaking more than two words, except to other 15-year-olds.

- Teenagers have to break a rule each day, and it works best if you let them get by with a minor one, even though it may be dyeing their hair navy blue or carrot orange—that is preferable to a tattoo.

- Survival depends mostly on patience and an elastic sense of humor for those bad moments that only seem funny days later.

If I had been 50, it might have been different, but physically I was down to one of everything: an ankle here, a bosom there, an eardrum lost somewhere in the middle of a noisy song by a rock group with an offensive name and song titles like "Do It, Do It, Do It." Again, lousy advice.

About this time, my book agent showed up to discuss a book I was doing on friendship. On hearing of my troubles, she advised: "Dump friendship, and do the kids."

She told me I was a statistic, that one out of four kids in this country is being raised by someone other than their parents. AARP has put in a hotline for surrogates. So, my third book emerged, *Unplanned Parenthood: The Confessions of a Seventysomething Surrogate Mother*.

One of the problems of aging surrogates is that you overworry, and you have a tougher time relating. My own children, now in their fifties, live on the West Coast, where they can be of no help to me whatsoever. But I call them for advice.

Once, I called to report that I was a little dotty in my role of recycled motherhood, and they promptly said in unison, "Mom, you always were dotty. Don't you remember the time you brought the wrong dog home from the vet?"

I was working at the White House at the time for a president who wanted everything done yesterday. The kids had a very fat Dachshund named "Mitzi," and I had left her at the vet and couldn't get back for two weeks. When I picked her up, they handed me a very skinny Dachshund, and I felt terrible. All the way home, I kept saying to her, "Oh, Mitzi, I am so sorry. Please forgive me." When I got home, I put her gently down on the grass. The kids came tumbling out of the house and shrieked, "Mommy, that's not Mitzi." I dashed to the phone and called the vet to see if they still had a mature-sized Dachshund. They did, and the switch was made. In my opinion, this could have happened to anyone. But my dog-loving friends don't think so.

However, that didn't end the telephone conversation. They also reminded me of the time I brought the wrong saint home. My husband's hobby was gardening, and he had wanted a statue of St. Francis of Assisi to put under the dogwood tree. Again, busy working mom, it was Easter eve when I dashed by a nursery to get it. There were about a thousand small statues of a man with a long robe, sandal shoes, and long hair. I grabbed one up—hopefully, not by the neck—paid for it and went home. Again, the kids came out, saw the statue, and shrieked, "That's not St. Francis, that's Jesus!"

Well, I'll let you in on a secret. You can't take Jesus back. No way. When I moved to Texas, I brought Jesus with me, and he is standing in my ivy bed. Now, with these teenagers, never have I needed him more.

Yet, I can't say that it was a negative experience. I have learned so much. My nephew tells me he is from the "orphan generation."

"Only one of my friends is living with both natural parents," he says. "The others are living with one parent and trying to keep peace between that one and another he visits." Or, he said, they live with neither parent, but with a grandparent or an aging aunt like me.

Today's teenagers are, in so many instances, the victims of divorce and are trying to escape a contentious world. The bounty from this situation is that we may be raising a generation more sensitive to diplomacy. (They often have to juggle two angry people, or they have to protect one parent from the other.)

They seem to me to be seeking solace in their music and in each other. I have observed, too, that this generation is color-blind and gender-blind. They have a head start on us in seeking justice, without the inhibitions that we inherited.

And a word for the English teachers. Most of them insist that today's teenagers keep a journal and, frequently, that journal is their only listener.

Am I glad I did it? Emphatically, yes. Not because it was a barrel of fun. Not because teenagers are grateful. That goes with the territory. When I feel oppressed, I have to ask myself, how many times did I say "thank you" to my mother? But I would rather do it, than fail to do it.

It has tested me in the winter of my life, and it has reassured me that I am—so far—strong enough to meet what life hands me. In some ways, it has been more challenging than the experiences of my past life, however vigorous and invigorating it was, because it has extracted more from me. And it has widened my knowledge of the '90s and the opportunities for a connection between the generations.

The words from the old lady in *Spoon River Anthology* come to me. She died at 96, after a full life, and she speaks to the people of the village from the grave:

> *"What is this I hear of sorrow and despair,*
> *Anger, discontent and drooping hopes.*
> *Degenerate sons and daughters,*
> *Life is too strong for you.*
> *It takes life to love."*

Unplanned parenthood IS about life.

A revered speech teacher once told me, "Begin as though you are taking off a pair of long kid gloves. You can't do that in a hurry."

—L. C.

16

ADVANCING YOUR APPEARANCE

In this chapter, I'll knit together the patchwork of details that sometimes are so obvious that they slip everyone's mind. The adage that "the devil is in the details" is true. Lack of attention to seemingly minute or obvious details has spelled disaster for many a speaker.

First, about honorariums. There are times when every successful speaker is asked to make an appearance *gratis*, and there are occasions when it is the right thing to do, such as for charitable benefits and other worthy causes. In earlier days, I sometimes spoke for love, for a massage, or for a freezer full of cookies. I still let my conscience dictate my fee, judging every invitation on its own merits.

If you don't have an agent, you can negotiate your own letter of understanding or contract. First, ask for the names of the last two speakers to address the group. If they were professionals, depending on the extent of their name identification, their fees will range anywhere from $5,000 (plus expenses) to $50,000, which Henry

Kissinger receives (plus a private plane ride), to $2 million, which Ronald Reagan received for his Japanese appearance. You can't get fees like that anymore.

If the last speakers were not well known—*Variety* calls them "Who Dats"—a polite way to ask the amount of the fee is, "What does your budget allow as an honorarium? Are travel and lodging expenses paid over and above that amount, or is that a flat fee?" If you know that the group can afford to pay you a fair honorarium, don't discount yourself—be upfront and firm. Say, "My minimum fee for speaking locally is $1,000," or "My usual fee for an out-of-town appearance is $5,000, plus expenses." At least half the time, they'll pay what you ask.

You'd be amazed at how reluctant program chairs are to mention cash. Yet you, the speaker, need to know whether it is worth your time to accept the invitation. The picture is improving, though, as more women are educated and progressive in their thinking. After decades of thinking that the giving of her time is part of a woman's civic duty, many women's organizations have had a rude awakening, and are finally coming around.

Once you've reached an agreement on the fee, tell the program director in advance what amenities you will need on the day of the event, and follow up your conversation with a phone call the day before to see if it was done.

Now, because I have a bum leg, it is important for me to make sure there will be a ramp, rather than stairs, leading to the stage or platform. You can minimize your handicaps with advance preparation.

Will you be seated at a table when speaking? Make sure it's skirted—avoid "overexposure!" And don't be shy about insisting on speaking from a seated position; more and more speakers—good ones—are doing so these days. If you are speaking from a standing podium, make sure it is the right height.

Regardless of whether you'll be seated or standing, make sure the microphone is mounted, not hand-held. A hand-held mike is cumbersome and makes it impossible to use your notes effectively.

Speaking of notes, there's no law against using them discreetly. Lay them before you in such a way that you can maneuver them easily, without catching the audience's attention. I always make sure that I have room to slide my pages to the side as I refer to them, rather than turn them noisily from a notebook.

Will the lights be dimmed during the speech? If so, you may not have enough light to read your notes. Ask the program director to provide an inconspicuous desk lamp. It's also important to ask that a spotlight be focused on your face. Your audience will pay closer attention to your words if your face is not just a distant blur, and your facial expressions are invaluable to the impact of your speech.

Be sure that you will have a poured glass of water, not a pitcher, and make sure it will be within easy reach. I began delivering a speech once without checking this out in advance. As I spoke, I began to look around for the water, and there—ten or twelve feet away from me at the far end of the table—was a beautiful silver pitcher with a lovely crystal glass beside it. Had I stopped midspeech to walk down to that pitcher, pour a glass of water, and walk back to the lectern, the audience would have been dozing by the time I returned!

How long do you have to speak? Don't believe it when they tell you "as long as you wish." Generally, anything over 30 minutes is too much. Hubert Humphrey was said to have been unable to sneeze in less than five minutes, so he had trouble with time constraints. Once, after having spoken for an interminably long time—and ignoring his staff's hand signals and discreet notes telling him his time was up—a member of the audience stood and said, "If you're having trouble with your watch, there's a calendar behind you!"

Make sure you write your speech to get your audience's attention from the very beginning. My reporting days in Austin coincided with Molly O'Daniel's wedding. Governor "Pappy" Lee O'Daniel had invited "everyone" to attend his daughter's wedding and have a piece of wedding cake. Well, "everyone" came and crowded the front yard of the Governor's Mansion, getting rowdy and raucous enough to demand some cake. Finally, Molly and the bridal party appeared with Pappy on the front porch, and, in the absence of any plan to distribute the cake in an orderly fashion, started breaking off hunks of it and tossing them into the crowd. Jack Gunn, a reporter for the now-defunct International News Service (the old Hearst Wire Service), wrote the lead we all wished we had written: "Pappy O'Daniel today went Marie Antoinette one better. He not only let the people eat cake, he threw it at them." That taught me a rule that has served me well through my lifetime of words, written and spoken: Hit 'em in the eye with the lead—who the hell reads the second paragraph?

Once you have composed your speech, write it and rewrite it, and move paragraphs on your word processor. Don't be afraid of recycling sure-fire anecdotes. Make sure your comments are appealing and convincing. Remove dated remarks about sensitive subjects such as race, sex, or sexual preference. About ten years ago, I had to discard what once had been a guaranteed laugh line, but would not play today: "Now, if I may deviate from my text without being a textual deviate . . ."

Mark up your copy: put slashes where you want to pause, underline words and thoughts that you want to emphasize, and make notes in the margin (*slowly, with feeling, spirited*).

And practice. There's no substitute for it. Stand in

front of the mirror and repeat your speech until it is your second skin. If, like me, you find the mirror distracting, deliver the speech to a friend who will tell you the truth and whose judgment you value.

Usually, I avoid formally acknowledging a lot of people at the beginning of my speech. It is brisker and more inclusive to say: "Mr. Chairman, Friends." Better still, have a little fun with the audience (you can do this more easily with specific types of organizations).

The size of the audience plays a part in determining the style of your delivery—whether it should be conversational or more formal. An audience of 50 or fewer invites an informal, personal style, as does the presentation of an award to a colleague, no matter what the size of the crowd. On the other hand, an event such as the dedication of a building or public monument might bring together a larger audience comprising people from all walks of life and would require a more formal tone.

Never determine the importance of your audience by its size.

And remember to vary the intonation of your voice. You can practice getting it right either by using a tape recorder and listening to yourself or by engaging a speech coach to help you. This is important! Monotone is a "sleeper."

One last thought: Don't give your prepared copy to anyone. The audience can't be attentive to your words and expressions if they are flipping through the pages of your speech as you talk. As incredible as it may seem, I even have seen instances where the speech text was printed in the program. How can you mesmerize an audience when they already know what you're going to say?

You'll need a supply of pictures and biographies to send to the program coordinator or publicity chairman. And they may come back to you and ask for an introduction for their program. Biographies are often too dull and academic. It is better to rewrite the bio to fit your audience. You may want to follow the lead of humorist Dave Barry, who writes and takes credit for his bio:

———————— ⟩⟩⟩ ⟨⟨⟨ ————————

DAVE BARRY
By Dave Barry

Dave Barry was born in Armonk, New York, in 1947 and has been steadily growing older ever since, without ever actually reaching maturity. He attended public schools, where he distinguished himself by not getting in nearly as much trouble as he would have if the authorities had been aware of everything. He is proud to have been elected "Class Clown" by the 1965 Pleasantville High School Class.

Barry went to Haverford College, where he was an English major and wrote lengthy scholarly papers filled with sentences that even he did not understand. He graduated in 1969 and eventually got a job with a newspaper named—this is a real name—*The Daily Local News* in West Chester, Pennsylvania, where he covered a series of incredibly dull municipal meetings, some of which are still going on today.

In 1975, Barry joined Burger Associates, a consulting firm that teaches effective writing to business people. He spent nearly eight years trying to get his students to stop writing things like "Enclosed please find the enclosed enclosures," but he eventually realized that it was hopeless. So in 1983, he took a job at the *Miami Herald*, and he has been there ever since, although he never answers the phone. In 1988, he won the Pulitzer Prize for commentary, pending a recount. His column appears in several hundred newspapers, yet another indication of the worsening drug crisis.

In 1996, Barry married Michelle Kaufman, a sportswriter for the *Miami Herald*. He has a son, Robert, who recently got his driver's license, which should make everybody nervous.

Barry has written a number of short but harmful books, including: *Babies and Other Hazards of Sex* and *Dave Barry Slept Here: A Sort of History of the United States*. His most recent books include *Dave Barry is NOT Making This Up, Dave Barry's Gift Guide to End All Gift Guides, Dave Barry Does Japan, Dave Barry Turns 40, Dave Barry's Only Travel Guide You'll Ever Need,* and *Dave Barry Talks Back*. His latest publication is a novel, *Big Trouble*. Barry's works have been hailed by critics as "containing a tremendous amount of white space."

Also, he owns a guitar that was once played by Bruce Springsteen.

(Dave Barry wrote this bio.)

———— ➡❘❘⬅ ————

With this technique, Dave has the audience laughing before he gets to the microphone.

You've apprised the program director in advance of everything you'll need, you've prepared a dynamite speech, and the big day has arrived.

If you are a woman, wear bright colors! If you wear white, you run the risk of disappearing into the wall; if you wear black, you may be indistinguishable among a sea of business suits. I recall former Secretary of Education Shirley Huffstetler who, after 15 years on the bench, said she felt like a "wicked woman" wearing anything except black. Her staff pleaded with her to wear bright colors when giving a speech, and they finally got her to relent to the point of wearing lavender—but that was as far as she would go! Even Al Gore had to forgo the dark suits for earth tones . . .

Do whatever it takes to look and feel your best. Have a manicure, or spend $50 to have someone do your hair and makeup on the morning of the event. It will be well worth it for the lift and confidence it will give you.

Don't arm yourself with a freshly typed copy of your speech. Take the dog-eared version that you've been practicing with, instead—it will be worn and familiar, like an old friend. Your delivery will be more effective if you have jotted helpful notes in the margins. I write myself reminders at appropriate points in the speech to coach me as I go, such as *"slowly," "pause,"* or *"don't cry!"* (at a place where I know I'm likely to tear up).

Get there early, and don't leave anything to chance. You are the only one who can appraise the room and its setup from your own unique perspective, so get there a half-hour to an hour before the event. Bring the list that you sent to the program director, and double-check everything yourself. Doing this has saved me from trouble many times.

When you arrive, find the program director and get him or her to take you to the room where you'll be speaking. Try to get a feel for the room—the more relaxed you are with your surroundings, the better received you will be by the audience.

Have someone go to the back of the room while you stand at the podium to make sure the microphone—and you—are at the right height. If the mike is too high, you'll look like you're peering at the audience over a fence, and you'll lose their focus. It may be necessary to make a quick dash to find a couple of heavy phone books to stand on.

How do you calm your nerves before you take the microphone? For me, it takes knowing that I have a secure blanket of words—marked up and practiced. I try to get a laugh line in at the start because laughter helps me to become a "ham," and signals acceptance by the audience.

When the time comes for you to deliver your speech, step up to the podium and look the audience over slowly. You want to feel at home with them. A revered speech teacher once told me, "Begin as though you are taking off a pair of long kid gloves. You can't do that in a hurry." Unite with your audience with your eyes, your smile and a sentence or two ("The last time I was here . . .") or a walk-on line that is a laugh line. Do not superimpose a joke unless it is relevant to the moment.

Finally, if there's a question-and-answer segment at the end of your speech, repeat each question as it is asked—this will help to make sure everyone in the audience heard it, and will give you time to think about your response. Answer the question directly—or evade in the most polite way you can.

One of the most difficult decisions a speaker has to make is deciding whether people who leave the room during a speech are vacating out of disgust or weak bladders.

—L. C.

17

THE HAZARDS OF SPEAKING

What's the worst thing that can happen to you while making a speech? Getting booed? Not getting any laughs? Dropping dead at the podium?

All of these things have happened to someone, so it is good to know what to do if you are at the mike and the unexpected occurs. My humor-writing friend, Bob Orben, advises three ways to go if a heckler boos you:

1. "Well, my friend, this is a democracy, and I believe the inarticulate should be given a chance to speak."
2. "'Boo' is such a strong sound—'boo' sounds like a cow with a speech impediment."
3. "There's a name for people who boo—all you have to do is to take 'boo' and add a 'b' to the end of it."

Whatever you do, don't invite the heckler to come up and speak. In fact, never relinquish control of your mike.

Jack Benny once had to contend with what most

humorists would consider the worst of all possible scenarios—he was getting absolutely no laughs. He was in "Back Bay" Boston, speaking to a very snooty crowd who never responded to his jokes. He kept straining for a laugh by reaching deeper and deeper into his cache of sure-fire laugh lines. Silence. When he concluded his remarks, he was desperate to leave town. As he gathered up his things to leave, a little lady with a high lace collar came up to him and said, "Oh, Mr. Benny, that was such a humorous speech. We could hardly keep from laughing."

One of the most difficult decisions a speaker has to make is deciding whether people who leave the room during a speech are vacating out of disgust or weak bladders. Once, at New York's Colony Club, I was warned by my hostess, Brooke Astor, "Don't go over 30 minutes. All of those on the front row start dropping their canes, as they head to the restrooms."

Once, while on the whistlestop trail in the wake of LBJ's controversial civil rights legislation, Lady Bird Johnson was confronted by the bigoted boos of some Columbus, South Carolina, residents who did their best to drown her out. Her method of handling them is a classic, and it worked beautifully. This gentle Southern lady raised her right hand to quell the noise and said, "Now that you have had your expression, let me give mine." The crowd applauded with such vigor that the Ku Klux Klanners cowed down and drifted away—only to meet us again in Savannah, Georgia, where she used the same tactic and received the same successful response.

On one occasion, Teddy Roosevelt was shot by a would-be assassin just as he reached the podium. The bullet was slowed down by his lengthy speech text, which was in his pocket. Teddy was not deterred. While the crowd looked on in horror, he said, "I came here to make

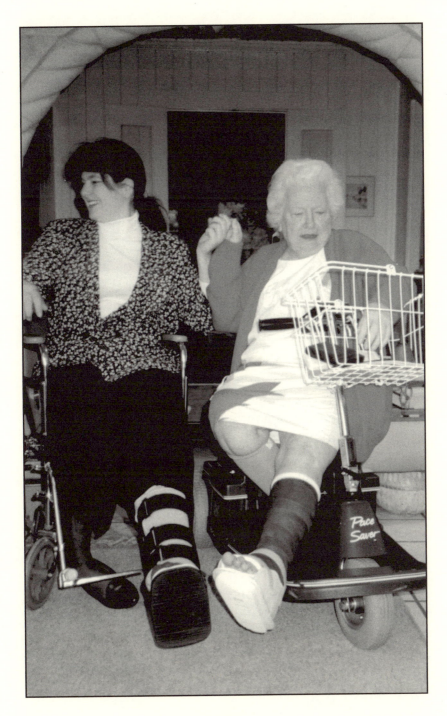

a speech, and that is what I am going to do." He proceeded to speak for more than an hour, bleeding all the while, and then was taken to the hospital for treatment.

Cactus Pryor, a popular Austin comedian and commentator, tells the sad tale of being introduced at a community event in a small Texas town. Just as the introduction ended, the emcee dropped dead! What did Cactus do? In his words, "I asked someone to call an ambulance, said a prayer over the corpse, and left town as quickly as possible. Funny thing, though, the widow felt an attachment to me and called me frequently for weeks afterward."

In some cases, dropping dead may be an appropriate exit. On April 30, 1956, U.S. Senator Alben Barkley collapsed and died of a heart attack at age 78 on the stage he loved best—the political platform. Barkley, who formerly was vice president in the Truman Administration, faltered and fell as he neared the end of a 30-minute keynote speech at Washington and Lee University's mock Democratic convention. He had just recalled his national political career as a Kentucky congressman, junior senator, senior senator, majority leader, vice president, and, finally, junior senator again. His last words were "I am willing to be a junior. I am glad to sit on the back row, for I had rather be a servant in the House of the Lord than to sit in the seats of the mighty." He stepped back, as though trying to continue, and fell, brushing a microphone to the stage with him. A hush fell over the stuffy gymnasium, which moments before had been rocking to Barkley's quips. Virginia's Governor Thomas B. Stanley escorted Mrs. Barkley to the platform, and a physician came to the fallen Barkley's side, but he was already dead. A minister who was on the stage said that he didn't believe the former vice president took "a single breath after he fell."

Drama—high drama—marked the speech of General Arthur MacArthur, father of General Douglas MacArthur, in 1912. I had heard the tale and wondered if it was true, but the account in *The General's General* tells the story, and it is worth repeating. The older MacArthur was one of the few remaining Civil War generals. His health had declined seriously due to high blood pressure and stomach ulcers. (He refused to give up cigars and Scotch whiskey.) He insisted on leaving his sickbed to speak at the 50th Reunion of the 24th Wisconsin Volunteers when the Milwaukee Chamber of Commerce held a dinner in their honor.

September 5 proved to be the hottest day of the year, and Wolcott Hall was stifling, even at 9:00 P.M. when the general arrived. The 64 remaining survivors of that once-proud company stood and gave him a tumultuous welcome of wild cheering for more than five minutes. After he was introduced by his old friend and comrade, Captain Edwin Parsons, the audience erupted again with a standing ovation lasting six or seven minutes.

"Comrades," MacArthur began, "little did we imagine 50 years ago that we would ever gather in this way. Little did we think that on the march to Atlanta so many of us would be spared to see Wisconsin again."

For ten minutes, MacArthur spoke of their battles. As he spoke of the battle of Peach Tree Creek, he stumbled over his words. The heat in the room was oppressive, and MacArthur's pallor worsened, as beads of sweat covered his face. The room fell silent. He leaned heavily on the podium and said slowly, "Comrades, I—am—too weak—to proceed."

He sank down in his chair, and his head fell forward to the table. He was dead. A blood vessel, weakened by 67 years of life, had burst at the base of the brain, and death was almost instantaneous.

Some comrades sobbed and began to say the Lord's Prayer. One of them removed a flag from the wall and draped it over his body. His old friend, Captain Parsons, who had introduced him, collapsed on top of the general's body, having suffered a paralytic stroke on his right side. An ambulance was called, and he died two weeks later.

Dropping dead at the podium is not a common occurrence, I'm happy to report. The hazards of speaking are generally much less fatal and can be avoided. Through the years, various speakers have used all manner of precautions and remedies to ward off the perils that threatened their speaking performances.

For instance, what do you do if you're hoarse on the day of the speech? You could use the "Sam Rayburn Remedy"—a jigger of Jack Daniels and a tablespoon of honey in a mug of boiling water. Sniff it and sip it slowly. Sam swore by it!

Leontyne Price had her own way of preventing hoarseness before a speech. She refused to allow air conditioning either in her car on the way to give a speech or in her hotel room preceding the address. Once, when the hotel's concierge had not complied with her wishes in advance, she draped her shawl over the A/C unit and called for management to bring a ladder to her room and turn it off.

One of the most difficult times to face an audience is when the original speaker has canceled and you have been brought in as a substitute. This happened to me when TV commentator Andrea Mitchell couldn't make it to the New York Women Life Insurance Executives meeting during the Bush Administration.

I hurried to San Diego to sub. What to open with? Here's how I decided to handle it:

Andrea Mitchell had to remain in Washington to cover the Great Broccoli Crisis, so I am the lucky one chosen to be with you today. I love replacing a younger woman who wears a size six.

I want to talk about your life and mine and how we can succeed as beneficiaries of the good lives we have been given...

A bad review can be a devastating thing for a speaker to handle. No matter how bad the review, handle it with humor. The worst review I ever received was from a *Washington Post* reporter who said, "Liz Carpenter sounds like a gym teacher on the *Titanic*." There were dozens of *Post* reporters who knew better than that, but the paper assigned one who didn't. The review was published on the morning that I was leaving on a nationwide book tour.

My husband was furious. He wanted to go punch the *Post* editor, Ben Bradlee, in the nose, but on the way to the airport we came up with a better solution. Our route led us by a nursery, where we stopped and purchased a large, phallic-like cactus that seemed to be waiting for our purposes. We paid $25 for it and dispatched it to Bradlee via taxi, along with a note that said, simply, "Thinking of you."

Somehow, all my anger subsided, and I laughed my way across the U.S., picturing the look on Bradlee's face when he received the cactus. Here and there, I stopped to mail him packages of fertilizer.

Bottom line—it's hard to win with a book critic who gets his nose out of joint with you. You just have to ignore those critics or come up with a graceful way to put them in their place.

Speakers need a supply of inspired quotes and funny lines. Someone once said: "Bad writers imitate; good writers steal." The best speechwriters learn quickly to keep a handy supply of quotes torn from newspapers, lifted off the Internet, or taken from notes scribbled while listening to another speaker. I do all of these.
　　　　　　　　　　　　　　　　　—L. C.

18

INSPIRED MATERIAL AND FUNNY STUFF

To write good speeches, you need to read good speeches. I keep two handy folders where I store quotes: one is marked "Inspired Material," and the other, "Funny Stuff."

Once, a lady came up to me in a parking lot somewhere in Georgia and asked me, "How can you be funny if you're just naturally morose?" It was that conversation that led me to include the following offering of "Funny Stuff" in this book.

It's true, some of us aren't natural comics and most of us aren't inspiring. But remember, the material doesn't have to be yours in order for you to capture the audience's attention. If you're not funny or inspiring, quote someone who is. That's legal, so long as you credit the originator: "As the late Erma Bombeck once said . . ." Or, if you can't remember (or don't know) the source, just admit that you don't know: "Someone once remarked . . ." As long as you don't take credit, it doesn't matter. Your audience will associate you with the humor, even if it's not your own.

My own speeches are peppered with humorous quotes from others. I have borrowed heavily from Erma over the years—and others.

So, my friends, I offer you up a bit of my own collection of "Inspired Material" and "Funny Stuff" that I have compiled over the years. Steal as you wish!

INSPIRED MATERIAL

Civilization is a web of cooperation joining people to family, friends, communities and country, creating in the individual, a sense of reliance on the whole . . . through powerful loyalties to the common good.   —BILL MOYERS

We think our civilization is near its meridian, but we are yet only at the cockcrowing and the morning star.
      —RALPH WALDO EMERSON

Those who do not know how to weep with the whole heart don't know how to laugh, either.   —GOLDA MEIR

In spite of illness, in spite of even the archenemy—sorrow—one can remain alive long past the usual date of disintegration if one is unafraid of change, insatiable in intellectual curiosity, interested in big things and happy in small ways.   —EDITH WHARTON

In all of us, there is a hunger, marrow deep, to know our heritage—to know who we are and where we came from. Without this enriching knowledge, there is a hollow yearning. No matter what our attainment in life, there is a vacuum, an emptiness and the most disquieting loneliness without it. —ALEX HALEY

The door might not be opened to a woman again for a long, long time, and I had a kind of duty to other women to walk in and sit down on the chair that was offered, and so establish the right of others long hence and far distant in geography to sit in the high seats. —FRANCES PERKINS

Governments can err, presidents do make mistakes, but the immortal Dante tells us that divine justice weighs the sins of the cold-blooded and the sins of the warm-hearted on different scales. Better the occasional faults of a government that lives in a spirit of charity than the consistent omissions of a government frozen in the ice of its own indifference. —PRESIDENT FRANKLIN D. ROOSEVELT

Change is not our enemy. On the contrary, society has no deadlier enemy than the refusal to change.
—PRESIDENT LYNDON BAINES JOHNSON

What is this I hear of sorrow and despair,
Anger, discontent and drooping hopes.
Degenerate sons and daughters,
Life is too strong for you.
It takes life to love.
—EDGAR LEE MASTERS
Spoon River Anthology

To have a stepping stone, you have to be willing to be one.
—MINNIE FISHER CUNNINGHAM

Against the onslaught of humor, nothing stands.
—MARK TWAIN

Long before I was struck with cancer, I felt something stirring in American society. It was a sense among the people of the country, Republicans and Democrats alike, that something was missing from their lives, something crucial. I was trying to position the Republican Party to take advantage of it, but I wasn't exactly sure what it was. My illness helped me to see that what was missing in society is what was missing in me. A little heart, a lot of brotherhood.

The '80s were about acquiring—acquiring wealth, power, prestige. I know. I acquired more wealth, power and prestige than most, but you can acquire all you want and still feel empty. What power wouldn't I trade for a little more time with my family? What price wouldn't I pay for an evening with friends? It took a deadly illness to put me eye-to-eye with that truth, but it is a truth that the country, caught up in its ruthless ambitions and moral decay, can learn on my dime.

I don't know who will lead us through the '90s, but they must be made to speak to this spiritual vacuum at the heart of American society, this tumor of the soul.
—LEE ATWATER
Former Republican
National Committee Chair

Women have been trained to speak softly and carry a lipstick. Those days are over.
—BELLA ABZUG
Saturday Review Press, 1972

It is not the critic who counts, not the man who points out how the strong man stumbles or where the doer of deeds could have done them better. The credit belongs to the man who is actually in the arena, whose face is marred by dust and sweat and blood; who strives valiantly, who errs and comes short again and again—because there is not effort without error and short-coming—but who does actually strive to do the deed; who knows the great enthusiasms, the great devotions, who spends himself in a worthy cause; who, at the best, knows in the end the triumphs of high achievement and who, at the worst, if he fails, at least fails while daring greatly, so that his place shall never be with those cold and timid souls who know neither victory nor defeat. —PRESIDENT THEODORE ROOSEVELT, 1910

When in doubt, do what is right.

—FRANCES PERKINS
(Quoting her grandmother)

While I am rocking you, my son, and singing lullabies,
Someone is planning stouter planes for death to ride the skies.
While I am dressing you, my son, in little boyish suits,
Someone is making uniforms and sturdy soldier boots.
While you are chasing butterflies amid the tangled grass,
Someone is testing chemicals to make a deadlier gas.
And while you eat your simple fare, perhaps the warlords sit
To start again the bugle note that only call the fit.
While I would build a splendid man, so fine and strong,
*   my son,*
Someone in secret tries to make a farther reaching gun.
A gun that on some distant day, when drums of battle roll,
May leave me with a golden star and anguish in my soul.

—MABLE FREER LOVERIDGE
"Foreboding"

Once, newspapers drew people to the public square. They provided a culture of community conversation. The purpose of news was not just to report and inform, but also to signal, to tell a story and to activate inquiry. When the press abandons that function, it no longer stimulates what the American philosopher, John Dewey, termed "the vital habits of democracy": the ability to follow an argument, grasp the point of view of another, expand the boundaries of understanding, debate the alternative purposes that might be pursued. —BILL MOYERS

There is a civil war in our society today, a conflict between two American cultures, each holding very different values. The adversaries are private profits versus public responsibility; personal ambition versus the community good; quantitative measures versus qualitative concerns.
—JOAN KONNER
Dean, Columbia School of Journalism

Among those whom I like or admire, I can find no common denominator. But among those whom I love, I can—all of them make me laugh.
—W. H. AUDEN

Washington—that great white marbled capital where good men do evil and evil men do good things in a way that only Americans can understand—and often they are baffled.
—ALLEN DRURY, Author
Advise and Consent

Do right and take the consequences.
—GENERAL SAM HOUSTON
First president of the Republic of Texas

Read your head off. —HARPER LEE
(Commenting on how
to learn to write)

*I suppose those dedicated to most crafts take pleasure in
the sights and sounds and smells peculiar to them, but I
can't imagine any being as exciting as the heavy odor of
printer's ink, pulp paper and melting lead, the clanking of
the old Linotype machines, the deafening din of clacking
news service printers, rewrite men shouting into the old
stand-up telephones—God, how I loved it!*
—WALTER CRONKITE

*America has a special meaning for me. I don't believe in
being hyphenated. We are all Americans, period.*
—HELEN THOMAS
Former dean of White
House correspondents

Let us remember Love, and each his own.
Love makes the serpent equal to the God.
It makes us larger than our flesh and bone
And lifts us from our jail of time and sod.

The wine, the roses, candle, violin
Are keepsakes in the musty books we save.
The kiss, embrace, the tingling of the skin,
All these delights are shadows in the cave.

And so, the games we play, the dance and search,
The pleasure, fame, the power and promotion,
Whether at market or home, in school or church,
Are passing mists and squalls upon the ocean
Of Love that gives us life till the last breath
And dying looks with that which knows no death.
—TOM SUTHERLAND

She attended the Nation's great needs,
Was admired by Persians and Medes,
But acquired, sad to say,
Somewhere on the way
An unhealthy attachment to weeds.

—HARRY MIDDLETON
Director, LBJ Library
(Toasting Lady Bird Johnson)

Life is an adventure or nothing at all.

—HELEN KELLER

'Tis not too late to seek a newer world: push off, and sit-
ting well in order to smite the sounding furrows.

—ALFRED LORD TENNYSON
Ulysses (Calling his friends
and shipmates to a
cooperative endeavor)

What must remain constant are the principles that must
guide all serious communicators. "Principles." That's the
key word. They will find that, as neophytes, they have
little strength with which to resist employers who are all
too frequently unprincipled. But, as diplomatically as pos-
sible in order to preserve their jobs, they should seek to
uphold the principles and persuade management to do
likewise. They should not hesitate to express their concerns
and convictions in those after-hour bull sessions that are
common to all offices. They will find more allies in their
company than even the old-timers may have recognized.

—WALTER CRONKITE
(His message to communicators
of the 21st century)

Journalism school began a search to learn about the won-
ders of the world and to pass them on. I felt that commu-
nications was a privilege I should regard with respect. I
didn't want to pass out material that was tawdry, ugly, or
trivial.

—LADY BIRD JOHNSON

The wind blew, and the crap flew, and we're all just here
for a day or two.

—PAT PAULSEN
(On life)

There's a song inside of me,
I can hardly wait to see
What it is I have to say
And the music it will play.

—THE REV. JAMES FORBES

Sometimes you don't have no control over the way things
go. Hail ruins the crops, or fire burns you out. And then
you're just given so much to work with in a life, and you
have to do the best you can with what you've got.

That's what piecing is.

The materials is passed on to you or is all you can afford
to buy—your fate.

But the way you put them together is your business.

You can put them in any order you like.

—MARY WHITE, Author
The Quilters

When someone treats you as his inferior, you can be sure that he no longer loves you, if indeed he ever did.

—CLARE BOOTH LUCE

It is odd that you get so anesthetized by your own problems that you don't quite fully share the hell of someone close to you.

—LADY BIRD JOHNSON
(On taking time to listen
to another person's anxieties)

I stand for motherland, America and a hot lunch for orphans.

—CAROL CHANNING

FUNNY STUFF

*Here's to the ability
To have the agility
To take your virility
Into your senility.*

—CARY GRANT

Our system is failing to solve the bedrock problems we face. One reason is that our public discourse has become the verbal equivalent of mud wrestling.

—BILL MOYERS

Life is a whole buffet table, and most of the idiots are starving to death.
—AUNTIE MAME

"Equality of rights under the law should not be denied or abridged on account of sex"—Look, ladies, those 16 little words simply mean one size fits all.
> —ERMA BOMBECK
> (On reading the proposed
> Equal Rights Amendment
> to the U.S. Constitution)

Ginger Rogers did everything Fred Astaire did. She just did it backwards and in high heels.
> —FORMER TEXAS GOVERNOR
> ANN RICHARDS

After the West Virginia primary of 1960, when JFK was accused of having his father buy the election, he read this mock telegram:

"I want to read you the telegram I received today from my father: 'Dear Jack. Don't go after Alaska or Hawaii. You don't need them, and I can't afford them.'"
> —PRESIDENT JOHN F. KENNEDY
> 1960 Gridiron Club Dinner
> Washington, D.C.

I remember a snowy night in Boston when the master of ceremonies didn't show up, and I had to introduce myself. I found accomplishments and character strengths that had never been mentioned before or SINCE.
> —AL CASEY
> Former chairman of American Airlines

From my kids, I have learned that it's better to give than to receive—and a hell of a lot more expensive.
> —ROY SPENCE

The mayor is just back from Japan. He didn't intend to go to Japan, but he got into the traffic on I-35 . . .

—CACTUS PRYOR

(Referring to Austin Mayor Kirk Watson and the city's burgeoning traffic)

The Pentagon Building was completed during World War II, and its hundreds of confusing corridors inspired jokes. There was the lady who ran up to a Pentagon guard and said, "Where's the door? Get me out of here quick—I'm about to have a baby."

The guard replied, "Lady, you should have known better than to come in here when you were pregnant."

"I WASN'T pregnant when I came in here."

—ANONYMOUS

I am happy to be here. I am really delighted to be here. If you believe that, I've got some land in northwest Arkansas I'd like to show you. Your club goes back to 1944, when Franklin Roosevelt delivered his fireside chats over radio. It's not much different today, except that you insist that the president sit directly on the logs.

—PRESIDENT BILL CLINTON

(Addressing a Washington press dinner during the Whitewater investigation)

There was a time when I could go for decades without thinking about my gums, but recently they loom larger in my mind than the greenhouse effect.

—DAVE BARRY

(On aging)

I've been criticized by quite a few people for making my brother, Bobby, attorney general. They didn't realize that I had a very good reason. Bobby wants to practice law, and I thought he ought to get a little experience.
> —President John F. Kennedy
> (On appointing Robert F. Kennedy attorney general)

If you owe a bore a dinner, send him one.
> —Alice Roosevelt Longworth
> (On entertaining)

And now, ladies and gentlemen, I want to thank each and every one of you who has helped me during the last four years. Thank you, Rosalyn.
> —President Jimmy Carter
> (At his final press dinner in Washington)

How do you calm your nerves before you take the microphone? For me, it takes knowing that I have a secure blanket of words—marked up and practiced.
—L.C.

19

CHEAT SHEETS FOR WRITING AND DELIVERING GREAT SPEECHES

On the pages that follow, you'll find a compendium of handy references that I hope will give you the essence of my philosophy of writing and delivering great speeches. Although some of them may seem elementary, I've found that many of them are things that you don't think of until you arrive at the gathering, and you're staring out at a room full of spectators, listening attentively . . . and realize it's too late to ask the questions and make the requests that will make your delivery more effective.

DOS AND DON'TS FOR WRITING AND DELIVERING SPEECHES

Do:
• To write good speeches, read good speeches.

- Have something of merit to say.
- Begin your speech with something to which both you and the audience relate.
- Pick the brains of the people who invited you for insight into whom you are addressing and why.
- If you're not funny, quote someone who is. It's legal, as long as you credit the source.
- Adjust your style to the size and type of audience—less formal for smaller groups or personal occasions, more formal for larger groups or public events.
- Keep two folders in which you save quotable quotes: "Inspired Material" and "Funny Stuff."
- Ask who comes before and after you in the speakers' lineup—this may provide a gag.
- Do your research. Dig for something that will make your speech inspiring.
- Use personal stories to lure the audience.
- Always check the quotes to be sure they're correct, attributed, and appropriate to the audience.
- When the purpose of your speech is to honor someone, use personal anecdotes to reflect on their humanity.
- When giving a eulogy, use your words to give the flavor of the person—not their résumé.
- Before preparing a commencement address, interview some of the graduates and read other commencement speeches.
- Try to add a human touch to high-tech speeches.
- Recycle your words and anecdotes.
- Mark up your copy: Put slashes where you want to pause, underline words and thoughts that you want to emphasize, and make notes in the margin (*slowly, with feeling, spirited*).
- Remove dated remarks about sensitive subjects such as race, sex, or sexual preference.

- When negotiating an honorarium, be upfront and firm. Ask for the names of the last two speakers to address the group, and ask what the budget allows for an honorarium. Don't short-change yourself.
- Have on hand several photos and a biography to send to the program coordinator or publicity chair.
- Ask for a spotlight to be focused on your face.
- Give the program director a written list of what you will need on the day of the speech.
- Write your own biography to fit the audience.
- Practice delivering your speech in front of a trusted friend.
- Use a tape recorder to practice intonation.
- Arrive at the location for the speech an hour early to get the feel of the room and make sure everything you need is there.
- Wear bright colors if you are a woman.
- Spend $50 on a manicure, hairdresser, or anything that will make you look and feel great.
- Lay your notes before you in a way that you can refer to them inconspicuously.
- Step to the mike and look the audience over slowly; connect with the audience by using your eyes, your smile, and a connective sentence or two, such as "The last time I was here . . ."
- Vary your intonation throughout your speech.
- Keep it short and to the point. Generally, limit your speech to 30 minutes or less.
- Get your audience's attention—and a laugh—from the beginning.
- Repeat questions before answering them.
- If you get a bad review, handle it with grace and humor.

Don't:

- Don't give your prepared speech copy to anyone in advance, except a reporter covering the events.
- Don't take a freshly typed copy of your speech—your well-worn practice copy will be much more familiar.
- Don't judge the importance of the speech by the size of the audience.
- Don't say "thank-you" at the end of a speech—generally, it's a downer; instead, let the tone of your voice say it in your closing remarks. Leave with an inspiring quote or a rallying phrase.
- Usually, avoid formally acknowledging a lot of people as you begin your speech. It is brisker and more inclusive to say, "Mr. Chairman, Friends," or something comical that is equally inclusive.
- Don't be stingy with the laughs.
- Don't be afraid to do something ridiculous to make the audience comfortable and win them over.
- When giving a welcome speech, don't highlight the area's main attractions—everyone knows about them.
- Don't speak in a monotone—it's a sleeper.

ADVANCING YOUR SPEECH
WITH THE PROGRAM DIRECTOR

- Give program director a written list of your requirements.
- Will there be stairs or a ramp leading to the lectern?
- Will you be seated at a table when speaking? If so, it should be skirted.

- Will you be speaking from a podium? Make sure it's the right height.
- Will you be able to have a spotlight on your face?
- Will the lights be dimmed during the speech? Ask for a small desk lamp so you can see your notes.
- Ask for a poured glass of water—not a pitcher and glass—within easy reach.

THINGS TO CHECK OUT
WHEN YOU ARRIVE

- Check the microphone to be sure it is at your level— have someone stand at the back of the room to make sure.
- Make sure the microphone is mounted, not hand-held.
- Check the lights, and make sure you have a desk lamp to read your notes, if the lights will be dimmed.
- Check the spotlight, if provided.
- Make sure there's a glass of poured water within easy reach.
- Arrange notes in front of you in such a way that they can be handled easily and inconspicuously.

Now, if you have read carefully, you know everything you need to know about sex and speeches. Go for it! Head for the speaking circuit, put yourself in front of the podium, grab the microphone and never let go. If this fails, you've still got sex.

—L. C.

PHOTOGRAPHS

*(All photos used in this book are
from Liz Carpenter's personal collection.)*

p. ix: The author's mother, Mary Elizabeth Sutherland, and Liz.

pp. xii-xiii: White House photo.

p. 6: Photo by Matt Lankes.

p. 11: With Elvira Crocker, who worked with Liz in the Department of Education during the Carter years.

p. 14: Advice from an aging neighbor. Liz with Emmett Shelton.

p. 16: Liz and President Bill Clinton, head to head at a Liz Carpenter Lectureship.

p. 18: Speechwriters aplenty, Johnson style. From left: unidentified White House aide, Liz, LBJ, and Joe Califano in 1968.

p. 21: A Harry Truman press conference—the days when the newswomen still wore hats. Liz is in a white hat on the first row, third from right.

p. 23: A kiss is just a kiss. President Clinton and Liz with Patty Lyon looking on.

p. 28: Backstage at a dinner in 1961. Liz and husband Les with LBJ and JFK.

p. 31: Dropping by the Bush White House. Christy Carpenter with mother Liz, Lady Bird Johnson, President Bush, and Mrs. Jake Pickle.

INDEX OF SPEECHES AND EXCERPTS

INDEX